HOMINIDS

First published in 2002 by
Grolier Educational
Sherman Turnpike
Danbury, Connecticut 06816
© **Quartz Editions 2002**

Library of Congress Cataloging-in-Publication Data
Extinct species.
        p. cm.
  Contents: v. 1. Why extinction occurs - - v. 2. Prehistoric animal life - - v. 3. Fossil
hunting - - v. 4. Extinct mammals - - v. 5. Extinct birds - - v. 6 Extinct underwater life - -
v. 7. Extinct reptiles and amphibians - - v. 8. Extinct invertebrates and plants - - v. 9.
Hominids - - v. 10. Atlas of extinction.
  Summary: Examines extinct species, including prehistoric man, and discusses why
extinction happens, as well as how information is gathered on species that existed
before humans evolved.
ISBN 0-7172-5564-6 (set) - - ISBN 0-7172-5565-4 (v. 1) - - ISBN 0-7172-5566-2 (v. 2)
- - ISBN 0-7172-5567-0 (v. 3) - - ISBN 0-7172-5568-9 (v. 4) - - ISBN 0-7172-5569-7 (v.
5) - - ISBN 0-7172-5570-0 (v. 6) - - ISBN 0-7172-5571-9 (v. 7) - - ISBN 0-7172-5572-7
(v. 8) - - ISBN 0-7172-5573-5 (v. 9) - - ISBN 0-7172-5574-3 (v. 10)
  1. Extinction (Biology) - - Juvenile literature. 2. Extinct animals - - Juvenile literature.
[1. Extinction (Biology) 2. Extinct animals.] I. Grolier Educational.

QH78 .E88 2002
578.68 - - dc21   2001055702

Produced by Quartz Editions
Premier House
112 Station Road
Edgware HA8 7BJ
UK

EDITORIAL DIRECTOR: Tamara Green
CREATIVE DIRECTOR: Marilyn Franks
PRINCIPAL ILLUSTRATOR: Neil Lloyd
CONTRIBUTING ILLUSTRATORS: Tony Gibbons, Helen Jones
EDITORIAL CONTRIBUTOR: Graham Coleman

Reprographics by Mullis Morgan, London
Printed in Belgium by Proost

ACKNOWLEDGMENTS

The publishers wish to thank the following for supplying
photographic images for this volume.

Front & back cover t SPL/J.Baum & D.Angus

Page 1t SPL/J.Baum & D.Angus;
p3t SPL/J.Baum & D.Angus; p8c NHPA/A.N.T.;
p9b NHPA/J.&A.Scott; p17tl NHM;
p21tc NHPA/D.Heuclin; p30-31bc OSF/S.Camazine;
p31t NHPA/A.Rouse; p32tr NHPA/A.Bannister;
p33t NHPA/D.Heuclin; p33br NHPA/D.Heuclin;
p35t NHM; p36-37c NHM; p39tl OSF/A.Huber/OKAPIA;
p39b NHPA/K.Schafer; p40 NHPA/G.Bernard;
p41tl MEPL; p41br NHPA/A.N.T.; p42bl OSF/J.Downer;
p43t OSF/S.Camazine; p43cr OSF/G.Willis;
p43bl OSF/D.Bromhall; p45tc MEPL;
p45cl OSF/S.Camazine; p45br NHPA/T.&T.Stack.

Abbreviations: Natural History Museum (NHM); Natural
History Photographic Agency (NHPA); Oxford Scientific Films
(OSF); Science Photo Library (SPL); bottom (b); center (c);
left (l); right (r); top (t).

EXTINCT SPECIES

HOMINIDS

GROLIER EDUCATIONAL
SHERMAN TURNPIKE, DANBURY, CONNECTICUT 06816

LOST AT SEA
Important ancient hominid remains once fell overboard while being transported from the part of the world where they were unearthed, as recounted on pages 20-21.

HUGE PREY
Some of the animals hunted by our ancestors were several times their size and would have provided meat for many meals, as you will discover on pages 28-29.

CONTENTS

Introduction   6
In which we outline the scope of this book that sets out to describe the search for human origins

Studying our ancestry   8
In which you can find out where paleontologists have dug for prehistoric human remains and the sort of information that these fossils provide

A false start   10
In which you will meet a creature, although only known from fragments of its jaw, that some once claimed was the oldest known hominid

Dug up in Africa   12
In which we invite you share the excitement of the team of paleoanthropologists who made a very important discovery on that continent

The story of Lucy   14
In which you can find out about the remains of a creature named Lucy by those who unearthed her skeleton

Homo habilis   16
In which a possible highly skilled ancestor of yours makes an appearance

Homo erectus   18
In which you will find information about the first species of hominid thought to have controlled and used fire

Peking man   20
In which you can read about the exciting discovery of fossil hominids in China at the beginning of the 20th century

Neanderthals   22
In which the surprising discovery of an ancient, humanlike skeleton found in a quarry in the Neander Valley, Germany, in 1856 is described

Cro-magnons   24
In which we present the so-called Red Lady, an ancient skeleton dug up in Wales, and later found to be the first *male* specimen of this species

HANDY HOMINIDS
On pages 32-33 you will discover how early types of hominids made and used tools like those shown here.

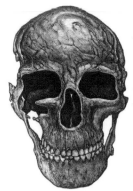

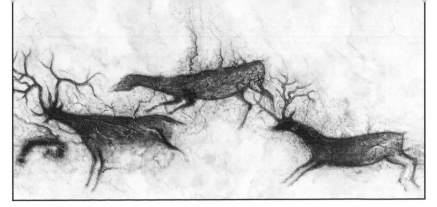

HEADLINE NEWS
Turn to pages 24-25 to find out which type of hominid had a skull like the one shown *left* and why its discovery made headline news.

Prehistoric art   26

In which we take a look at cave paintings and consider what they reveal about the lifestyle of early humans

Early hunters   28

In which the attempts of primitive human predators to catch and kill are described

Cracking the code   30

In which we take a look at the evidence provided by our genes to show we may share a common ancestor with chimpanzees

Early tools   32

In which we present some of the primitive instruments used in ancient societies for hunting and building

Man-beasts   34

In which curious creatures which might be throwbacks from prehistoric times are featured

The Piltdown hoax   36

In which you will find the amusing true story of a trick that was played on paleontologists

Primitive societies   38

In which we look at what paleoanthropologists have discovered about the daily lives of the early hominids

Challenges   40

In which you are invited to consider for yourself various theories about human evolution

Saving humanity   42

In which we look at the many dangers facing us in the world today and what might be done to avoid them

Future Man   44

In which we hazard a guess as to how *Homo sapiens* might evolve over millions of years

Glossary   46
Set index   47

ON THE WALL
Cave paintings reveal a lot about those animals hunted by our ancestors, as described on pages 26-27.

HAIRY HOMINID
Would this hominid have looked so different from today's humans if he had shaved and put on a modern suit? Turn to pages 22-23 to find out.

INTRODUCTION

BORN FIGHTERS
The Cro-Magnons, shown *above*, first evolved in the Middle East but then traveled west and fought with and overcame the Neanderthals.

Fossilized remains show that many different species of *hominids*, or members of the human family, existed in the distant past before, finally, modern mankind, known by scientists as *Homo sapiens sapiens* (meaning "Man the wise"), evolved. Lucy, for example, found in Ethiopia, is one of the earliest fossilized skeletons of an upright-walking hominid to have been unearthed. Her bones had lain buried for millions of years, but soil erosion eventually brought them to the surface where they were discovered in 1974. These skeletal remains revealed that little Lucy – she was only about 4 feet tall – was an *Australopithecus* (O̲-STRAH-LOH-PITH̲-EK-US.)

When, though, did the earliest hominids start to stand erect and to walk on two legs? What was their level of intelligence? And in what sort of communities did they live?

ON FIRE
Some scientists believe that the hominid *Homo erectus* was the first to use fire for keeping warm and for cooking.

LANDMARK DISCOVERY
Remains of *Homo habilis,* one of the first of our ancestors to use tools, were discovered in Tanzania, Africa, in 1964.

Scientists can tell a lot about their lives, which diseases they suffered from, how they made and used tools, and how closely they resembled us simply by studying their bones and surviving artifacts. But why did each type of hominid finally die out? And most importantly, what might we need to consider if we are to save modern human beings from risk of extinction? There is much food for thought within the pages of this book.

GENERAL INTELLIGENCE
Well-preserved remains, such as this skull, provide important clues about the mental capacity of the various types of hominids.

LIVING TOGETHER
Our prehistoric ancestors did not dwell in small family units but in larger groups, sharing caves or other primitive forms of shelter.

STUDYING OUR ANCESTRY

Not everyone accepts the biblical creation story literally. That is why scientists known as *paleoanthropologists* (<u>PAL</u>-EE-OH-AN-THROP-<u>OL</u>-OH-JISTS) spend time trying to find out when and how we humans evolved on this planet.

A CLOUDY ISSUE
Where on Earth, seen here in a view from outer space, did our forerunners evolve? Some scientists think the earliest hominids first appeared on the African continent, but others believe it may have been in Asia.

What makes you, as a modern human being, a unique species? You walk on two legs, only crawling on all fours during early infancy; you have a larger brain than other mammals; you have a more flattened face and a more prominent nose than the apes; you are not covered with a full coating of body hair; you are the only mammal to sweat so profusely; and you have a spoken and written language.

More than this, however, as a member of the human race, you are very adaptable and able to exert more influence on the environment than any other creature that has ever lived or that exists today.

THE HOMINID LINE

Many present-day scientists now suggest that, millions of years ago, humans and modern chimps may have had a common ancestor. This does not mean you have evolved from a chimp, however. Instead, the descendants of this common ancestor may have evolved along two different paths, one progressing to become modern chimps and the other evolving into a group known as hominids, to which you belong. Scientists include all creatures which lived along our evolutionary line, including modern human beings, in the category *hominid*. The common ancestor, meanwhile, which is thought to have existed is known as the "missing link."

Although scientists differ about how long our species has existed, if we do all have a common ancestor, this means all human beings alive today are related. You, your neighbors, and people living on the other side of the globe may therefore be distant cousins.

The most exciting thing about the science of paleo-anthropology is that lots of evidence no doubt still remains to be unearthed. But how do those scientists who look for fossils of early hominids set about their painstaking work?

Some paleoanthropologists obtain clues as to where they might make further finds of hominid remains by reading the research papers, technical magazine articles, and academic books produced by those who share this profession and who have already been successful in unearthing hominid fossils or who have interesting theories.

But some of these scientists may be based elsewhere in the world – one reason why it is useful for paleoanthropologists to understand at least one foreign language. Cooperation between paleoanthropologists is essential if further knowledge about our likely ancestors is to be gleaned.

Satellite images and aerial photographs can also indicate likely locations to begin digging for hominid remains; but, of course, permission is always required from landowners or the government of a particular country. Some hominid fossils have even been spotted on the surface of open, barren land, where they had been left undisturbed for eons.

After these fossils are recovered, they must be cleaned, pieced together because many remains are often badly fragmented, and then studied. Now read on and find out about some of the most exciting landmark discoveries ever made in the field of paleoanthropology.

Fact file

● In 1994 a team of paleoanthropologists led by a University of California scientist, Tim White, found remains in Ethiopia, eastern Africa, which they thought came from our earliest human ancestor and named it *Ardipithicus ramidus* (ARD-IP-ITH-IK-OOS RAM-EE-DUS.)

● Later, however, Ethiopian scientists found even older remains of bipedal creatures with the teeth of hominids which have been dated to over 5 million years ago.

● More recently, in 2000, French scientists claimed to have found a hominid in Kenya dating from 6 million years ago, but further research is required to prove this. We are continually finding out more about our earliest ancestors.

IN SEARCH OF FOSSIL EVIDENCE
The photograph, *below*, shows the paleoanthropologist Richard Leakey, one of a family renowned for their life-long quest to find fossil evidence of human origins. He is seen beside a pile of burning ivory, an antipoaching measure to save the African elephant.

A FALSE START

Scientific opinion differs as to whether a creature known as *Ramapithecus* (<u>RAM</u>-AH-<u>PITH</u>-EK-US) was really an early hominid. Some say it *was* one of our distant ancestors; others think it was *not*. Read on, consider the evidence, and then draw your own conclusions.

Paleoanthropologists have long talked about trying to find the "missing link" – a fossil that might show humans and apes once shared a common ancestor. Indeed, many thought this absent piece of the fossil record had at last been discovered when in 1932, remains of a particular ancient creature were unearthed. The fossil evidence was very incomplete, however, and comprised only a few bits of jaw and teeth belonging to what must have been a small animal weighing no more than 40 pounds. Nevertheless, the fragments – dating from between 12 and 14 million years ago – were enough for some scientists to suggest that *Ramapithecus*, as it was later named, was possibly bipedal and the earliest of our ancestors. Arguments against this theory, meanwhile, centered on its teeth.

BONES OF CONTENTION

At first, some scientists thought the creature named *Ramapithecus* by American scientist, Dr. G. E. Lewis, who first studied its remains, was a hominid and looked like the illustration *left*. But most now consider it was *not* our earliest ancestor after all.

CHANGE OF OPINION

A few years later, the discovery in Turkey and Pakistan of two *Sivapithecus* fossilized skulls gave added weight to the views of those who held that neither of these creatures was a direct part of the hominid line. Even though *Ramapithecus* may well have had a short, deep hominidlike face and relatively small teeth, and whether or not its remains were actually those of a *Sivapithecus*, the majority of scientists now agree it was essentially apelike.

Professor Arunachalam Kumar, an anatomist from India, has recently come up with an equally controversial theory. He believes that creatures like *Ramapithecus* and *Sivapithecus* may even have survived to this day in some inaccessible regions of the world. Their presence, he says, may explain the occasional reported sighting of the so-called yetis, almas, and other

Those who maintained that *Ramapithecus* was *not* a hominid were quick to point out there is a living African ape with small teeth just like those that had been found. They were adamant, too, that on the basis of a few fossilized teeth it could not be proved the creature walked upright. When a complete *Ramapithecus* jawbone was dug up in 1976, many other scientists reached the same conclusion. It was clearly not a hominid, they said, but probably belonged to the apelike species, *Sivapithecus* (<u>SEEV</u>-AH-<u>PITH</u>-EK-US).

Fact file

- The facial characteristics of modern human beings probably began appearing around 100,000 years ago. Before that, early hominids still looked very apelike.

- The name *Ramapithecus* means "Rama's ape." This creature was named after the Hindu deity Rama.

- *Sivapithecus* is named after the Hindu god Siva. The orangutan is thought to be descended from *Sivapithecus.*

- *Sivapithecus* and *Ramapithecus*, whether or not separate species, were probably mostly quadrupedal, moving about on all fours rather than standing upright.

- An apelike creature called *Proconsul* (<u>PROH</u>-KON-SOOL) was an ancestor of *Ramapithecus.*

strange-looking beasts in remote parts of the Himalayas, China, Vietnam, and elsewhere in Asia. But only if a live or recently deceased specimen is ever found will those who have declared these throwbacks to be nonexistent or mere figments of the imagination be proved wrong.

Dug up in Africa

In his book *The Descent of Man* 19th-century British naturalist Charles Darwin predicted that if ever the earliest ancestor of human beings was discovered, it would be in Africa. In 1924 a scientist from another continent seemed at first to have proved him right.

NAMED WITH A SENSE OF FUN
This reconstructed skull of an *Australopithecus africanus* is similar to the one found by Raymond Broom in 1947, which was nicknamed Mrs. Ples.

When Raymond Dart, a young Australian, unearthed in a limestone quarry at a place called Taung in South Africa 2-million-year-old bone fragments, he was immediately convinced they were part of the skull of a creature that must have been fairly human in appearance, even though he named it *Australopithecus africanus*, which means "African southern ape." Dart, however, was met with suspicion. He was criticized, for instance, for choosing a name that was difficult for the public to pronounce, and for mixing words of Greek and Latin origin in this name.

But more significantly, the scientific establishment of the time, and the public at large, were not ready to be presented with such an apelike supposed ancestor, and so were shocked by his conclusions. Indeed, it was to take about 30 years before his idea became more widely accepted.

BABY FACE

The remains had clearly belonged to a child, later known as the Taung baby, even though it was at least four years old. The skull showed it must have held a brain the size of a juvenile ape's, but there were far smaller canine teeth in the jaw than those of young gorillas or chimpanzees. Dart also thought the skull's base must have supported the spinal column of a creature with an upright gait.

Among some of the remains found in southern African caves by Dart were skulls of baboons that had clearly been killed by predators. He therefore decided that *Australopithecus* must have been a carnivore.

One of the best preserved *Australopithecus africanus* skulls ever discovered was found by Robert Broom, a colleague of Raymond Dart and a supporter of his theories, in a cave at an area called Sterkfontein, near the town of Johannesburg, South Africa. The teeth belonging to this adult hominid indicate it must have been an omnivore. Scientists also think the skull came from a female, and have chosen to name her Mrs. Ples. Remarkably, her cranium had not broken up over time. The skull seemed to have become separated from the rest of her body and then to have rolled below an overhanging rock. This saved the skull from being crushed from above.

BIGGER AND STRONGER
This illustration of a typical *Australopithecus robustus* skull shows it had a larger head structure than the type known as *africanus, top,* probably due to differences in diet. They were contemporaries, however.

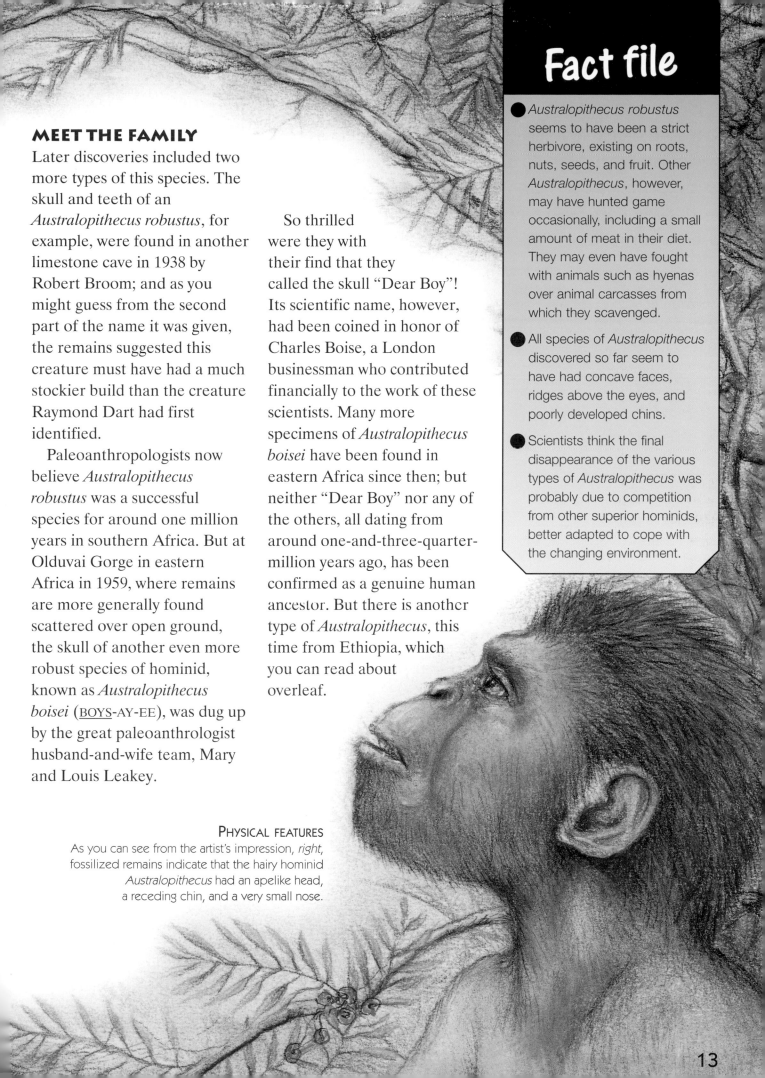

MEET THE FAMILY

Later discoveries included two more types of this species. The skull and teeth of an *Australopithecus robustus*, for example, were found in another limestone cave in 1938 by Robert Broom; and as you might guess from the second part of the name it was given, the remains suggested this creature must have had a much stockier build than the creature Raymond Dart had first identified.

Paleoanthropologists now believe *Australopithecus robustus* was a successful species for around one million years in southern Africa. But at Olduvai Gorge in eastern Africa in 1959, where remains are more generally found scattered over open ground, the skull of another even more robust species of hominid, known as *Australopithecus boisei* (<u>BOYS</u>-AY-EE), was dug up by the great paleoanthrologist husband-and-wife team, Mary and Louis Leakey.

So thrilled were they with their find that they called the skull "Dear Boy"! Its scientific name, however, had been coined in honor of Charles Boise, a London businessman who contributed financially to the work of these scientists. Many more specimens of *Australopithecus boisei* have been found in eastern Africa since then; but neither "Dear Boy" nor any of the others, all dating from around one-and-three-quarter-million years ago, has been confirmed as a genuine human ancestor. But there is another type of *Australopithecus*, this time from Ethiopia, which you can read about overleaf.

PHYSICAL FEATURES

As you can see from the artist's impression, *right*, fossilized remains indicate that the hairy hominid *Australopithecus* had an apelike head, a receding chin, and a very small nose.

Fact file

- *Australopithecus robustus* seems to have been a strict herbivore, existing on roots, nuts, seeds, and fruit. Other *Australopithecus*, however, may have hunted game occasionally, including a small amount of meat in their diet. They may even have fought with animals such as hyenas over animal carcasses from which they scavenged.

- All species of *Australopithecus* discovered so far seem to have had concave faces, ridges above the eyes, and poorly developed chins.

- Scientists think the final disappearance of the various types of *Australopithecus* was probably due to competition from other superior hominids, better adapted to cope with the changing environment.

THE STORY OF LUCY

One of the oldest hominids so far discovered was an *Australopithecus*, dubbed the mother of us all and given the name Lucy, even though scientists cannot be certain the remains are definitely those of a female. What is known about this possible ancestor?

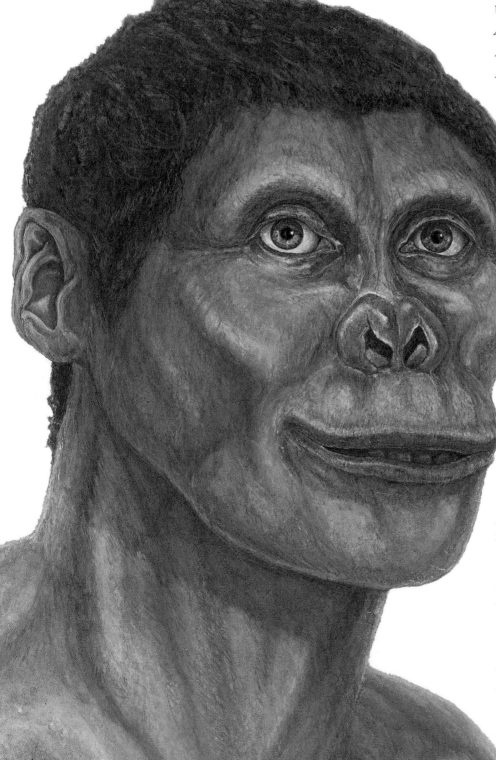

Lucy was given this name because the Beatles' song *Lucy in the Sky with Diamonds* happened to be playing when American paleontologist Donald Johanson brought the skeletal remains back to his camp site. Johanson also gave this species the scientific name *Australopithecus afarensis*, after Afar, the region of Ethiopia, Africa, where she had been discovered.

We know from the fossilized bones that Lucy was just 4 feet in height, and that she probably lived about three million years ago. Her pelvis was so small that scientists disagree over whether she was in fact a woman because the pelvic structure of a female hominid is usually far broader and so more suitable for child-bearing. However, it is also difficult to tell from the skeletons of chimpanzees whether they were male or female since their pelvic bone structure is so similar; so perhaps this was the case with both sexes of *Australopithecus* too. It is the sort of prehistoric enigma that may never finally be solved.

FACIAL FEATURES

This portrait of Lucy has been painted as a result of studying the remains of her skull. However, she may have been more masculine in her looks and even, as some scientists have suggested, male.

When scientists laid out the remains of Lucy's small skeleton, *left*, they reached the conclusion that when she was fleshed out, chances are she only weighed about 66 pounds.

What some experts suggest we must bear in mind, however, is that Lucy was probably no more entirely representative of her species than any one individual of the world today. Some of us are short, some tall, some slim, some fat.

FLOOD VICTIM?

How, though, did Lucy meet her death? Because her skeleton was not completely destroyed, many scientists think she had not died as the result of an encounter with a wild animal, as the so-called Taung child is thought to have done. Instead, they put forward the theory that she may have perished in a flash flood. In Lucy's time Ethiopia would have been a far wetter place than today; and torrential rain may have been a frequent occurrence.

Most of her skull was missing when Lucy was unearthed. Nevertheless, scientists have a fair idea of what she must have looked like. From other parts of her skeleton, for example, they can tell that she had short legs, long arms, and slightly hunched shoulders.

Fact file

● At the same site where he had found Lucy, Donald Johansen later unearthed further fossils of hominids who may perhaps have been member's of Lucy's immediate family. There were 13 individuals in all. Four were infants under 5 years of age, as shown by their teeth,and the rest were juveniles and adults. The differences in height, however, may mean that the find included different types of early hominid.

● Lucy's hands and shoulders suggest that she may have spent some time in the trees as well as on the ground.

● The discovery both of Lucy and the *Australopithecus* footprints proved hominids walked upright at least 3,500,000 years ago.

But what actually suggests to the evolutionists that Lucy was one of our ancestors? In 1978 very interesting tracks of others of Lucy's species were found in volcanic ash at a place called Laetoli in Tanzania, Africa. They show an arched foot, a structure that is entirely unique to hominids.

The prints were later covered with sand to protect them from weathering, but contained acacia seeds which sprouted and finally grew over these trace fossils. In 1993, however, the prints were unearthed. There were 29 in total, and all were left at the site after casts were made and photographs taken of these relatives of Lucy.

HOMO HABILIS

In 1961 at Olduvai Gorge in Tanzania, Africa, scientist Mary Leakey discovered the skull of a previously unknown hominid, later named, when further remains had been found, *Homo habilis,* meaning "skilful man," because the hand structure showed great dexterity.

Together with her husband Louis, Mary Leakey made several fascinating finds during the time they were working at Olduvai Gorge; but their son Richard's team unearthed even more exciting remains 11 years later at another African site – the older and badly fragmented but eventually more complete skull of another *Homo habilis.*

It was an important discovery, but weeks of patient, very exacting work were required to fit together the hundreds of pieces. Indeed, this task must have been like completing the most complex jigsaw puzzle you can imagine. The task of fitting it together fell to Richard Leakey's wife, Meave, the anatomist Dr. Bernard Wood, and others.

HANDY MAN
Homo habilis, shown here using a tool, is thought to have been more skilled at using his hands than any previous or contemporary hominid.

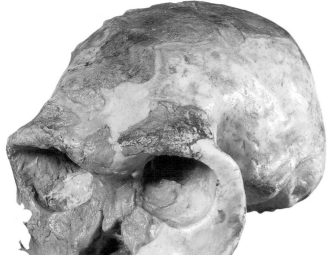

In his autobiography *One Life*, Richard Leakey describes how they set about assessing the size of this hominid's brain.

"Gradually a skull began to take shape and we began to get a rough idea of its size. It was larger than any of the early fossil hominids that I had seen, but the question was, how large was the brain? We decided to attempt a crude guess. Beginning by carefully filling the gaps with Plasticine and sticky tape, we then filled the vault with beach sand and measured the volume of the sand in a rain gauge."

It took about 6 weeks to reconstruct the skull, and it turned out to have about half the cubic capacity of one belonging to a modern human being. This led scientists to the conclusion that *Homo habilis* must have had limited intelligence. However, this species had a larger brain than the hominid *Australopithecus*, alongside whom it lived some 2,800,000 years ago.

Leakey's skull was not given a name when it was found and has not been given one since. Instead, it is always referred to by the number 1470, which is simply its catalogue reference in Kenya's National Museum, where it is now kept.

Most scientists think that *Homo habilis* was one of the first hominid species to use tools to butcher animals for food about two million years ago, as depicted in the illustration shown *far left*. However, when the opportunity arose, members of this species may also have scavenged, taking what meat remained on the carcasses of any dead creatures that they happened to find when going about their daily lives. It is not hard to imagine the babble and signing that might have been used to convey to others in the group that they had found the remains of a creature such as a deer, from which a meal could be prepared for them all. However, the fossilized teeth of *Homo habilis* show that this hominid was probably an omnivore, and would have eaten many sorts of vegetation as well as flesh.

PIECED TOGETHER
The illustration *below* shows the skull, known simply as 1470, which was found by Richard Leakey and his team by Lake Rudolf in Kenya. His wife worked painstakingly to reconstruct it.

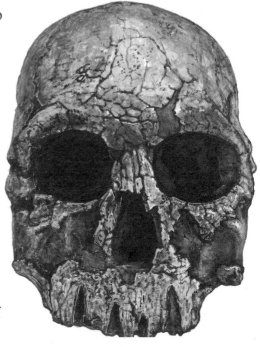

Homo erectus

Possibly the first hominid to discover how to make and use fires and among the earliest to leave Africa for Asia, *Homo erectus* is likely to have developed far superior communication skills to those hominids who preceded him and even his contemporaries.

Homo erectus, with a scientific name meaning "upright man" and who was descended from *Homo habilis*, had a brain about three-quarters the size of yours which indicates a fair level of intelligence. Visible differences included a backward-sloping forehead and stocky build.

This species of hominid first came to the attention of paleontologists when the 19th-century Dutch scientist Eugene Dubois went to the island of Java, Indonesia. Here, Dubois found the skull of a *Homo erectus*; and then the following year, he unearthed a thigh bone. We now know from fossilized remains that *Homo erectus* evolved in Africa about 1,750,000 years ago but that the species later migrated to live in many different parts of the world.

HIGHBROW HOMINID
As this fossilized *Homo habilis* skull shows, among the main facial characteristics were a thick brow ridge above the eye sockets and big teeth.

Homo erectus must have found life very different when he moved from Kenya, Africa, and began to inhabit more temperate regions. After this hominid reached Europe, for instance, he had to get used to the four seasons as well as restricted food supplies during winter months. Mastering use of fire no doubt helped keep him warm and he was now able to cook the animals he caught when hunting.

AROUND THE FIRE
Having discovered many of the uses to which fire could be put, *Homo erectus* probably ate and kept warm in groups, as shown here.

Homo erectus is also known to have had good tools for chopping and cutting, and probably ate communally. One particularly interesting specimen, found in Kenya, shows diseased bone, due to excessive Vitamin A. It is a rare condition, but the most usual cause is huge intakes of liver. So this unfortunate individual may well have eaten far too much of this animal organ.

When examined under a microscope, however, the tooth patterns of several *Homo erectus* show that, as well as meat, they also ate roots and tubers.

Many scientists are also convinced that these hominids could communicate with a basic form of speech. Their vocabulary probably only consisted of a few simple words; but whistles, cries, grunts, and facial expressions, would have sufficed.

Fact file

● *Homo erectus* probably lived a nomadic life, which is how over the years this species came to occupy entirely new regions.

● Scientists believe that *Homo erectus* was dark-skinned, its pigmentation providing the species with extra protection against harmful ultraviolet rays from the intense sunlight of Africa. Earlier species would have been protected by their thick body hair.

● Axes and cleavers were principal items in the *Homo erectus* toolkit.

● The original name given to this hominid was *Pithecanthropus* (PITH-EK-AN-THROP-US) *erectus*, meaning "upright ape-man."

● The most complete *Homo erectus* skeleton found so far is 1,500,000 years old.

PEKING MAN

In the 1920s at a cave site in China, remains were discovered that lent weight to the idea that humans may first have evolved in Asia. Now, however, we know that they were over two million years younger than the oldest African hominid remains discovered so far.

In China during the early part of the 20th century, it was possible to buy fossilized animal teeth which had been unearthed to be ground down to fine powder and used to treat a whole variety of ailments. Then, to everyone's surprise, a few teeth which seemed to have belonged to primitive humans were found.

Dr. Davidson Black, who was a professor of anatomy at the time, studied these teeth and also other remains which he believed had once belonged to a species with a resemblance to the hominid *Pithecanthropus*. Commonly called Java Man, this species had been discovered by the Dutchman, Professor Eugene Dubois, in Java, Indonesia.

Extensive excavations soon began at site near Peking (now Beijing) where the Chinese fossils had been found; and in all by 1937 the skeletal remains and teeth of more than 30 males, females, and children of the species were discovered.

Like *Pithecanthropus*, so-called Peking Man is thought to have had an erect posture but this species was probably not as strong as Java Man, to judge by fossil evidence. However, the two species probably had a similar way of life; and their fossilized teeth, the remains of animals, and fruit found near their own fossilized bones show that they were both omnivores, eating meat and vegetation. Smashed skulls found at both sites, meanwhile, indicate the two species perhaps became cannibalistic when food was in short supply.

Both species probably lived in tribes consisting of about 30 individuals; and because they would have needed to communicate, it is likely that both Java and Peking Man spoke, using a very simple form of language.

In 1941, when war between Japan and China had reached a crisis point, scientists in China became so concerned about the remains of Peking Man that they decided a group of American marines, about to embark for the United States, should take the fossils with them for safekeeping. As things turned out, however, this decision was not a wise one.

MADE TO MEASURE
This skull is a copy of one belonging to Peking Man which disappeared at sea. Fortunately, detailed descriptions of its structure survive.

The ship on which they sailed sank, and none of the crew survived. The skeletons of these marines therefore probably still lie at the bottom of the ocean, alongside the packing cases in which the fossils of Peking Man had been so carefully packed.

LOST OVERBOARD
In 1941 during World War II many important remains of Peking Man were lost when the ship carrying them to the United States for further scientific study sank somewhere in the Yellow Sea. The fossils have never been recovered.

Fact file

● The first remains of primitive humans to be found in China were unearthed in the caves of a place called Dragon Bone Hill, not far from Beijing.

● Peking Man was first known by the scientific name *Sinanthropus pekinensis* (SEYE--NAN-THROH-PUS PEK-IN-EN-SIS), meaning "the Chinese man from Peking." Today, however, this species is called *Homo erectus pekinensis*, meaning "upright man from Peking."

● Although the former existence of *Sinanthropus pekinensis* was first based on just a few fossilized teeth, several complete skulls and jaws were eventually unearthed.

● Excavations have shown Peking Man was a hunter and knew how to use fire.

NEANDERTHALS

We do not know for certain why the Neanderthals disappeared from our planet about 35 thousand years ago. But what has been discovered about their appearance and way of life? Where have their remains been unearthed, and how did they get their name?

The name *Neanderthal* comes from the *Neander* Valley near Düsseldorf, Germany, where this hominid's remains were first discovered in 1856. As a limestone quarry was being blasted, workmen suddenly noticed a few curious-looking bones among the rubble, including part of a skull with particularly heavy brow ridges and some bowed leg bones.

At that time and in certain circles today, it was contrary to general religious belief that these humanlike remains could have been much more than 6,000 years old. If they had been older, it would have meant they predated Adam and Eve, the first human beings according to biblical tradition.

One German scientist therefore came up with another suggestion, claiming that the leg bones must have belonged to a Russian Cossak who had spent too much time on horseback – hence his bowed legs!

Another scientist thought the skeletal remains might have belonged to a man suffering from rickets. People who have this disease develop soft and bowed bones due to a lack of Vitamin D in their diet. Others thought the bones might have belonged to someone from some unknown modern race. But all of these theories were, of course, completely wrong.

Similar skeletons were later dug up at La Naulette and Naumur in Belgium; and even more bones were subsequently found in a small cave at La Chapelle aux Saints and Le Moustier in France.

Together, these remains have given scientists a fair picture of the Neanderthals who, as we now know, lived in Europe between 100,000 and 35,000 years ago. There is evidence, too, that they also inhabited countries such as Israel in the Middle East as well as parts of North Africa.

COMPARE AND CONTRAST
The illustration, *left*, shows Neanderthal bones being examined at the quarry where they were first dug up in the 19th century. Look at the two figures, *right*, for a comparison between a Neanderthal and a modern human.

AN INFLEXIBLE VIEW

About 100 years ago the French paleontologist Marcellin Boule was asked to reconstruct a Neanderthal from some remains, but he made a lot of mistakes when he undertook this task. First of all, he gave the model a spine that was not very flexible.

MAKING PROVISION
Using wood and animal skins, the Neanderthals built shelters where there were no caves. They were also probably intelligent enough to provide for the future by storing water, perhaps in the shells of hatched ostrich eggs.

This meant that his Neanderthal walked with a stoop. He also arranged the foot bones so that his Neanderthal would have walked on the outside of his feet. No wonder everyone who saw his model thought the Neanderthals must have been very like apes! Only as recently as 1957 were these errors recognized and corrected.

We now know from a footprint found in Italy that Neanderthals probably had wide but flat feet and that they walked upright. Neanderthals had foreheads that sloped backward at the top and receding chins. The males and the females were also probably far hairier than we humans are today.

Fact file

● Neanderthals lived at the time of a great Ice Age and so had to cope with harsh conditions. However, their stocky build meant they had considerable fat reserves to keep them warm when temperatures were very low.

● This hominid had probably discovered how to tie logs together to make a raft and so cross rivers.

● Excavations have shown the Neanderthals buried their dead with many types of plants, as well as tools and food, in the belief that the deceased would need sustenance for a future life of some kind.

● Some people think that hairy creatures seen in remote parts of Asia and known as *almas* may be surviving Neanderthals.

A bone from the base of a Neanderthal's tongue, found on Mount Carmel in Israel, shows that they were capable of speech; and scraping tools provide evidence that they knew how to prepare wild animals for food and clothing. They probably lived peacefully until, that is, they encountered a species you can read about on the two pages that follow.

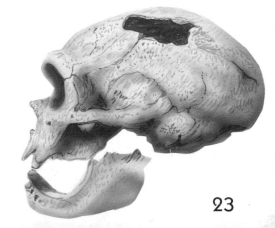

DEAD AND BURIED
This skull of a Neanderthal was dug up from a burial site at La Chapelle aux Saints in southwest France. Experts have put his age at around 45, not very old by today's standards but elderly for a Neanderthal.

CRO-MAGNONS

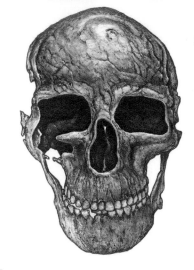

About 35,000 years ago, from the Middle East came hominids known as Cro-Magnons, who looked very much like humans do today. They may well have come face-to-face with the Neanderthals, finally either wiping them out or possibly interbreeding with them.

Cro-Magnons lived at around the same time as the Neanderthals for a few thousand years. But while the Neanderthals dwelt in Africa and Europe, the Cro-Magnons at first lived in the Middle East, and then migrated to the West. Some scientists even think that Cro-Magnons may have invaded Neanderthal territory, and that these two species frequently fought with each other over land.

BIG AND BURLY

The Cro-Magnons were quite a bit taller than Neanderthals, reaching 6 feet in height and had large hands and feet. It has also been suggested they were less hairy than the Neanderthals. In fact, in many ways Cro-Magnons looked even more like today's human beings. They are thought to have been far more intelligent than the Neanderthals too and to have made better weapons.

THEN AND NOW
The Cro-Magnon skull *above* is very much like the skull of a contemporary human being, but has been dated to approximately 30,000 years ago.

The first discovery of this hominid – consisting of a male skull and the remains of a woman, two other men, and a baby – was made in the 1860s in a cave known as Cro-Magnon, in the Dordogne region of western France, hence the name of this species.

WHO BEAT WHOM?
This illustration shows a group of Cro-Magnons in battle. Can you identify their opponents? Who were the likely victors?

The skull was of a man aged around 50 when he died and has since been described as belonging to the "old man of Cro-Magnon." The woman seems to have had a head injury, but signs of healing show she probably lived for a while after the accident.

When these remains of Cro-Magnons were first unearthed, they were immediately accepted by the scientific community as possible ancestors of modern human beings. Their fossilized bones showed they must have looked very much like we do and their facial features in particular were similar to ours.

Some scientists, however, think Cro-Magnons may may not have wiped out the Neanderthals entirely but that they interbred. Eventually modern humans, with the scientific name of *Homo sapiens sapiens*, may have evolved.

If that is the case, then all of us alive today – yes, *you*, too – may actually carry both Neanderthal and Cro-Magnon genes and may be descended from them! Just imagine, some of your ancestors may well have taken part in a battle between Neanderthals and Cro-Magnons exactly like the one shown in the illustration *below*!

PREHISTORIC ART

Bison, horses, oxen, ibex, mammoths, deer, and bears – all have been found depicted on the walls of prehistoric caves. Indeed, some of our ancestors seem to have been very talented artists. What materials did they use? And why did they choose to paint wildlife?

Small statuettes of women, probably carved over 30,000 years ago, have been found all over Europe. They are thought to have been fertility symbols and are known as Venuses. Numerous other figurines and decorative ornaments from this period have been unearthed, too. But most interesting of all are the examples of cave art that have survived.

SHEDDING LIGHT

Naturally, it would have been very dark within such caves. How, then, did the cave artists manage to see what they were doing and draw with such skill? The remains of more than 75 very early lamps found at one site provide a clue.

These primitive lamps were made of slabs of stone. Into them, a hollow depression was introduced and this was then filled with animal fat which would be burnt to shed light just like a candle. It is also assumed that the cave artists must have erected scaffolding to help them reach and decorate the ceilings and highest parts of cave walls.

Possibly the most famous site where such paintings have been found is the Lascaux cave in southwest France. Here, bold illustrations of all sorts of animals are thought to have been made 14,000 years ago. Some are huge, and some are small; but all are very colorful.

Particularly striking is the fact that the images found in this cave are full of movement. These are not static portraits. Instead among them you will find trotting horses, a jumping cow, running deer, and a racing bull, for instance.

But were these paintings – outstanding even by modern standards – an example of art for art's sake and purely decorative? Or could they perhaps have had some other purpose?

Fact file

● Most cave paintings were produced on the walls of readily accessible caves; but some have been found very far underground.

● The very first discovery of decorated caves was in 1879 at Altamira in Spain.

● Cave artists did not depict themselves but painted the animals that they hunted.

● Not all cave paintings are confined to Europe, although most have been found there. Some rock paintings were produced by Australian Aborigines and are more than 20,000 years old. Handprints made 2,000 years ago by Native Americans have also been found on a rock face at the Natural Bridges National Monument in Utah.

Rich purples, blacks, reds, and yellows feature very prominently. These pigments would have been obtained from natural earth colorings which were ground down and then mixed with fat, not water, to judge by the excellent state of preservation of these murals. The paint was probably applied to the walls straight from the fingers. But the very simplest brushes made from chewed sticks or animal fur may also have been used. There is even evidence it may have been blown through tubes onto the cave walls at times.

Experts agree that caves such as the one at Lascaux were probably not living quarters but areas set aside specifically for communal meetings or for prayer. Indeed, one theory as to why almost all cave art features beautifully depicted animals but only crude, "matchstick" humans is that they were possibly depicted by our ancestors as part of a series of mysterious sacred ceremonies performed prior to a hunt. During these, the deities may have been shown the sort of prey they hoped to round up and kill, in the hope that the gods would provide a successful outcome.

EARLY HUNTERS

Scientists believe that way back in time our ancestors had the appetites of carnivores, killing many different species of animals for their meat and sharing the kill among the community among which they lived.

Early humans faced a constant struggle to find enough food. Before toolmaking and hunting expeditions were common they depended almost entirely on scavenging. This meant stripping the carcasses of animals that had either died naturally or been killed by stronger predators; and before fire was used for cooking they would have eaten raw flesh.

Chasing animals on foot – even after sharp implements came into use – would have been not only tiring and risky, but also time-consuming.

But our ancient ancestors soon became wily enough to set traps. A deep hole would be dug in the ground and covered with plant material.

The aim was that unwary animals would walk across the vegetation, stumble into the pit, and be unable to escape. Such a method of hunting was very ambitious. If a huge woolly mammoth, for example, could be trapped in this way, there would be sufficient meat, hide, and fur to provide food and clothing for a great many people for a considerable time.

But some hunters may have been brave enough to chase or goad a large beast into a pit or over a cliff. Others no doubt drove or goaded their prey into swamps or deep snows, where they would get stuck and so become easier to kill. Whole tribes may even have taken part in this.

SNEAKY HUNTERS

At other times humans may have disguised themselves by dressing up in animal skins and crawling on all-fours. Then they would sneak up on their prey until within striking distance. Some early humans may even have stalked herds of migratory animals such as reindeer so that they were assured of a food supply. Indeed, our primitive ancestors would almost certainly have been experts in recognizing and following animal trails. Then, after they had caught up with them, the youngest and weakest of the pack would be picked off first or individuals isolated from the pack for slaughter.

Catching fish may have been important too; and short spears would have been used by our ancestors to stab at larger river or marine victims, or reeds were woven into primitive nets.

TAKE-OUT FOOD
On occasions, hunters would have found dead animals purely by chance. Provided they got there before any other scavenger, they could then carry away the creature, as shown *left*, to be cut up and devoured.

IN DISGUISE
Our distant ancestors are thought to have been wily and may even have camouflaged themselves in animal skins so that their prey would be less wary.

Boys may have hunted with the men, and we can assume that, in groups, they would have chased and then used scaled-down versions of the adults' tools to catch small game. We can also hazard a guess that boys played a part by driving animals into pens, where the adults would take over and go in for the kill.

Birds were probably caught either in snares or by the simple method of throwing rocks. It may also be that animals were sometimes hunted not for food but for mysterious ritual reasons, perhaps as sacrifices to the gods or simply as trophies to demonstrate our ancestors' hunting prowess. Many animal skulls found in caves in Switzerland seem to bear this out.

Fact file

- At a site in France paleontologists discovered a large collection of horse remains dating back 17,000 years. It seems these animals were driven over a cliff during a mass hunting expedition.

- A collection of 250,000-year-old elephant bones found in Spain suggests early humans hunted these, perhaps by driving them into swamps, and then maybe ate them.

- Prehistoric cave paintings of reindeer, bison, and horses are thought to indicate these creatures were popular prey.

- Our very earliest ancestors were probably not carnivores but gatherers, with a diet of nuts, plants, fruits, roots, eggs, and any other edible matter readily available.

DANGEROUS MOMENTS
It was far safer for our prehistoric ancestors to scavenge for food, but sometimes they would risk their lives against huge prey.

CRACKING THE CODE

Paleoanthropologists still hope to strike lucky and find definite fossil evidence for the "missing link," said to be an ancestor of chimpanzees and modern humans. Meanwhile, biologists have broken a code which shows both species have a similar genetic makeup.

The oldest secrets in the world lie hidden in the cells of every type of living organism. However, we human beings did not fully understand the implications of this until the 1950s, when scientists Francis Crick and James Watson announced they had succeeded in breaking the genetic code.

The secret – a microscopic archive of inherited instructions or messages for the formation and function of all living things – is carried in the nucleus of each live cell and is known as DNA, an abbreviation for the scientific term *deoxyribonucelic acid* (DEE-OX-EE-REYE-BOH-NOOK-LEE-IK ASS-ID.)

Your body comprises billions of cells; and in just one DNA molecule there are about three billion genes, half inherited from each parent, which control our characteristics.

At high magnification DNA looks like two strands twisted together in a spiral (known as a "double helix.") Amazingly, if the strands in a single, tiny, barely visible cell were stretched out in a line, they would extend to about three feet in length. The two strands are like a ladder, and are joined by rungs which scientists refer to as "base pairs" – the genes or coded messages which make you the way you are.

In effect, genes provide the instructions for everything in nature – from the color and patterning of a butterfly's wings to the length of your nose, or the color and texture of your hair or the size of your feet.

What is particularly interesting is that comparison of human and chimpanzee DNA shows we are very close to the chimps in our genetic makeup. We are therefore very likely to have had a common ancestor in the distant past. From our point-of-view, however, this does not mean we once looked exactly like chimps do now; nor, from a chimp's point-of-view, does it mean they once looked like us.

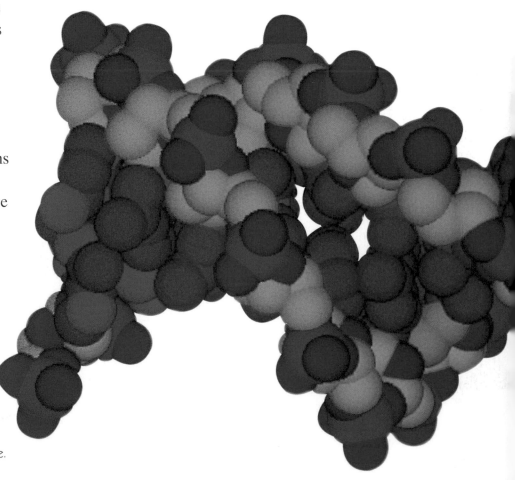

BLUEPRINTS FOR LIFE
The so-called double helix of each of the body's billions of DNA molecules, shown *right*, carries a huge number of different chemical patterns or genes. These are the coded messages making each of us the individuals that we are.

Remarkably, study of the DNA of humans and chimps has shown that the very small, 1.7% difference in our genetic makeup gives us very different features.

Another kind of chemical known as *mitochondrial* (MEYE-TOH-KON-DREE-AL) DNA, however, exists *outside* the nucleus of each cell and is passed down only through the female line.

Studies have revealed greater differences in this type of DNA among people of African origin than those of us whose ancestors seem to have come from elsewhere on the globe. The suggestion has therefore been made by some scientists that mitochondrial DNA may have had more of a chance to evolve among those of black African origin simply because it existed for longer in that part of the world. In other words, one school of thought has it that hominids may indeed first have appeared on that continent.

Fact file

● According to one branch of scientific thinking, the physical differences that exist between people who come from various parts of the globe only arose as recently as 50,000 years ago. *Homo sapiens sapiens* is said to have developed Chinese, African, Asian, or Caucasian features at that time due principally to prevailing environmental and climatic influences.

● Sometimes the genetic instructions in our cells can become damaged and as a result are not copied perfectly for the next generation. This sort of change is known as a *mutation*. Usually, a mutation is very small and goes unnoticed. But it may be significant enough to cause a sudden jump in evolution.

A FEMALE LINK

Some scientists even think the ancestry of *Homo sapiens sapiens* should be traced back to one woman, rather than a man, who lived in Africa about 200,000 years ago. She has been nicknamed Mitochondrial Eve, after the mitochondrial DNA that is passed on only through the female line. So will it be biologists, now they have cracked the code, or a team of paleoanthropologists who find certain evidence for the so-called missing link? Debate about this continues.

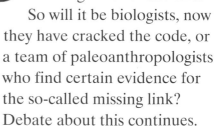

Early Tools

After our forebears became sufficiently skilled, they no doubt carried their own sets of weapons for self-protection against wild creatures. But remains show axes, spears, and arrows were crafted for other distinct purposes too.

Paleoanthropologists agree that even a creature as primitive as *Ramapithecus*, once thought by some to have been an early human ancestor, probably used any stones of adequate size and weight found lying about to make the simplest of implements. This most basic of prehistoric tools, a piece of stone struck with another to provide a sharp, cutting edge, is known as a "flake" and was first made nearly three million years ago.

Flakes could be held comfortably in the hand, were tough, and would last a very long time. Indeed, such stone tools were so useful that our ancestors continued to make them for over a million years.

But one paleoanthropologist, Raymond Dart, claimed in 1949 that split animal bones and teeth predate the use of stone tools, and many scientists now agree with him, pointing also to the use of branches as levers.

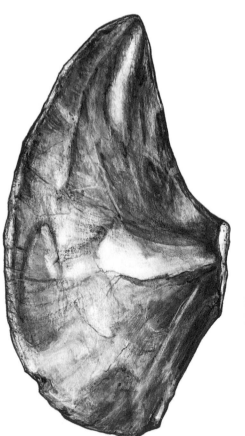

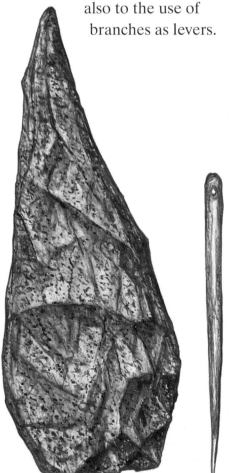

FLINT STONES
Arrowheads like those shown here and formed from flints would have been used by primitive hunters to kill their prey, perhaps as long as 30,000 years ago.

In time the design of more sophisticated tools made hunting possible. Axes and flints could also be used to skin and then carve up dead animals found on scavenging missions. Our ancestors' diet therefore became more varied.

Meat and bone marrow are highly nutritious, so that our ancestors grew stronger and healthier, also living longer lives. Good food helped us to develop larger brains, too, so that we became more intelligent.

Over many thousands of years, we also became sufficiently skilled and hardy to dare to travel long distances and find new hunting grounds.

Some experts even believe toolmaking encouraged early humans to leave the continent of Africa where, some say, we first evolved and to spread around the globe.

Many such early, sharp stones have survived in places such as Africa, the Czech Republic, Denmark, Russia, France, and China, as have teeth, tusks, and antlers, shaped into implements for building shelters, or making jewelry or baskets. Some carry the marks of blows and cuts; and examples of primitive needles, the eyes made with small, stone drills so that they could be used for sewing clothes made from animal skins, have also been unearthed. To find out how such tools were used, paleoanthropologists have looked to the Aborigines of Australia, the Bushmen of Africa, North American Indians, and the Eskimos because even in comparatively modern times, some of their tools have been very much like the most ancient ever found.

HOW TALENTED ARE YOU?
Do you think *you* would be skilled enough to make tools like those shown *left* from the simplest of raw materials, as our long-lost ancestors did?

IN A SUPERB STATE
This flint hand-axe is probably around 40,000 years old and was found in France. For its age it is in remarkable condition.

MAN-BEASTS
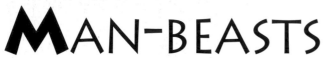

Every now and then, there are supposed sightings of creatures that resemble us in some respects but are not entirely human in appearance. Could they be throwbacks to our prehistoric ancestors, or are they merely figments of the imagination?

A strange animal looking a little like *Homo erectus* because of its protruding jaws and ridged brow, and dubbed the yowie, has been reported to be living in remote parts of Australia. By coincidence, it has been spotted near to places where the remains of hominid fossils have been unearthed.

Similar creatures have in fact been seen in many parts of the world. The yeti (also known as the abominable snowman), for example, is said still to inhabit the Himalayas. According to those who have caught sight of it, this creature has a conically-shaped head, is about 5 feet in height, and has a body entirely covered with reddish-brown hair. Only rarely does it leave its preferred forest environment. Skeptics, however, suggest that it might not be a hominid but a large species of orang-utan or some other ape or monkey.

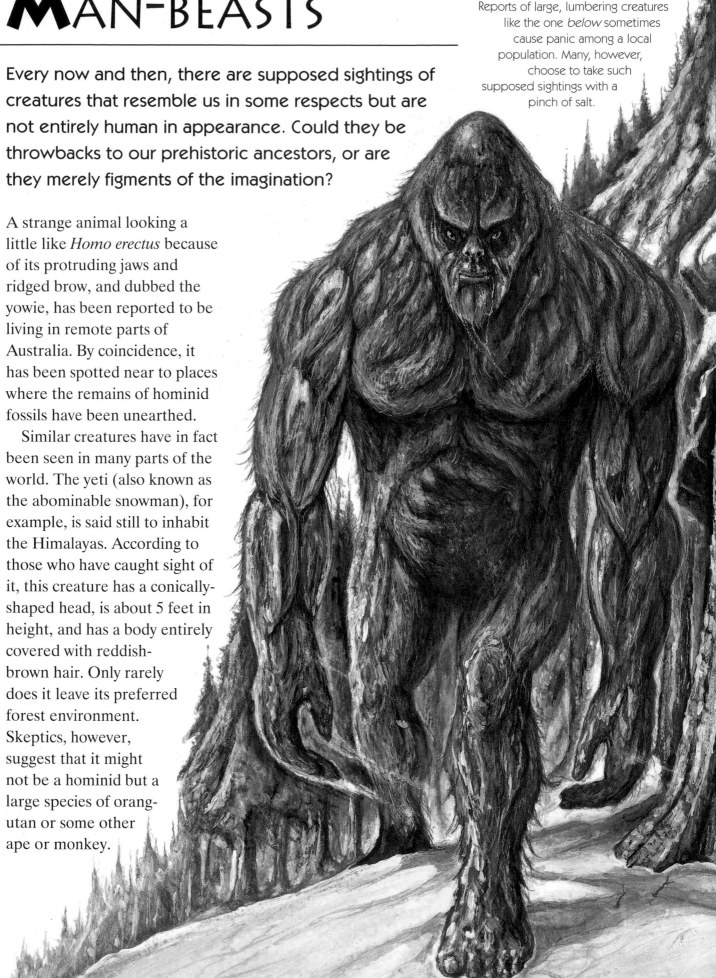

FALSE ALARMS?
Reports of large, lumbering creatures like the one *below* sometimes cause panic among a local population. Many, however, choose to take such supposed sightings with a pinch of salt.

SURPRISE APPEARANCES
Might long lost species thought to be our ancestors not be extinct after all?
Reported sightings of Neanderthals or other hominids appearing
out of the blue present this as a possibility but firm proof has yet to be found.

One Tibetan lama (or priest), meanwhile, claims to have examined the mummified corpses of two creatures known locally as *rimis*. They, too, are said to have looked very much like humans but were very hairy and about 8 feet tall. The mystery deepens because remains of *Gigantopithecus* (JEYE-GAN-TOH-PITH-EK-US), thought by some scientists to have been an early ancestor of ours and by others to have been a gigantic ape, suggest a remarkably similar appearance to that of the rimis. However, *Gigantopithecus* is said to have died out 300,000 years ago. It is odd, too, that a man-beast reported to roam remote parts of North America and dubbed bigfoot also bears more than a passing resemblance to *Gigantopithecus*.

JUST FOR SHOW

One such creature, nicknamed Bozo, is even said to have been shot in the skull during the Vietnam war and to have been smuggled into the United States. It was then encased in ice to preserve it for public exhibition as part of a fairground sideshow in Minnesota during the 1960s. But many people, including the FBI, reached the conclusion it was a fake, constructed and displayed purely for monetary gain. Some scientists, however, remained convinced it was an authentic specimen.

Whatever the truth, this corpse was eventually replaced by a model and the original seems to have disappeared.

ON ROCKY GROUND
Do mermaids exist? Those who claim to have seen one usually find themselves on rocky ground because most scientists would put them down to nothing more than a mere mirage or optical illusion.

THE PILTDOWN HOAX

Back in 1912, there was great excitement in the scientific world. Many paleontologists agreed that at long last fragments of the fossilized skull and teeth of a "missing link" between humans and apes had been discovered. But there was a huge surprise in store.

In its issue for December 28, 1912, the highly respected journal *The Illustrated London News* proudly announced that the Geological Department of the British Museum was putting on display the remains of what was said to be the most ancient inhabitant of Great Britain, if not the whole of Europe. These fossils had been unearthed one year previously in a gravel pit near to Piltdown Common in the county of Sussex, England.

A MISSING LINK?

Everyone was truly astonished at this remarkable find, particularly as the fossil was said by the reporter to be from *"a link with our remote ancestors, the ape,"* and to date back several hundreds of thousands of years.

Entirely by chance, the remains, shown *right*, had been discovered by attorney Charles Dawson who also had an interest in archaeology; and before long many of England's scientists were speculating as to what Piltdown Man must have looked like and the sort of life he would have led.

TAKEN IN

The *Illustrated London News* for December 28, 1912, featured the *above* illustration of what some scientists thought Piltdown Man may have looked like. Now, of course, we know it was all a hoax.

Fact file

● The Piltdown skull had been fashioned in such a way that, to us today, it looks like the skull of an *Australopithecus*; but this hominid was not in fact discovered until later.

● A book entitled *Piltdown: A Scientific Forgery* by Frank Spencer, published in 1990, names the scientist Sir Arthur Keith as the chief suspect of the hoax.

● At the time when the Piltdown hoax took place, hominids were thought by many scientists first to have evolved in Asia. No remains had yet been found in Africa.

● Even the Keeper of Geology at the British Museum of Natural History was fooled into accepting the specimen as genuine at first.

They even named the early large-brained hominid *Eoanthropus dawsoni* after Charles Dawson.

Piltdown Man was thought to have been short and to have had a brain twice twice the size of that of the highest apes. He was described as a hunter, and experts even went so far as to hazard a guess that he might have included elephant and rhinoceros meat in his diet.

But not everyone was agreed. *The American Museum Journal,* for instance, was far more circumspect and in 1914 reported that a number of important paleoanthropologists believed the specimen could not possibly be genuine. They even went so far as to suggest in print that the remains might have been *"artificially fossilized and planted in the fossil bed, to fool the scientists."*

Scientists have shown that bones of the same age from the same deposits will contain the same amount of fluoride, but these remains did not.

A CLEVER FAKE

As it turned out, the skeptics had been right. But not until 1953 was the skull finally identified as human and no more than 500 years old. It had been made to look far older by clever use of staining.

The jaw bone, meanwhile, was found to have belonged to a modern orangutan; and the wear on the teeth had been produced by a file. The planting of this artificial fossil had clearly been a deliberate hoax. Yet to this day, no one is entirely certain whether Charles Dawson and the experts had been fooled or whether Dawson himself was perhaps the perpetrator.

PRIMITIVE SOCIETIES

Back in prehistoric times, were there family groups like today, or was communal living more common? What part did women play in everyday life? Where did our ancestors shelter? And what sort of religious practices were there? Paleoanthropologists have found several clues to the way our ancestors lived.

After our ancestors had learned to make fire – using it for warmth, light, cooking, and to keep wild animals at bay – it is likely they regularly used it as a central gathering point. The ability to control fire therefore played a key role in bringing primitive humans together in tribes or extended family groups.

FEW HOME COMFORTS
Caves provided a natural source of shelter for our ancestors. When it was cold, some early humans even put up screens or tents of animal skins at the entrances to keep the warmth in and unwelcome animals out.

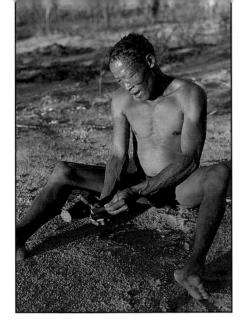

CARRYING ON
The Bushman, *left*, from Namibia in southern Africa, still leads the traditional life of a hunter-gatherer, similar to that of our distant ancestors.

LEARNING TO SPEAK

The other major factor that turned our forebears into social creatures was the development of speech. Early humans no doubt first just experimented with sound. But then, as they spent more time in the company of others, they would have begun to give names to everyday objects and to express such feelings as anger or delight. Language, however basic, must have gone a long way toward helping our ancestors feel part of a community. Indeed, scientific experiments have also shown that language – even simple signing – is best learned in a group environment. With fire and speech our ancestors could now begin to live more ordered lives. They could share food and plan ahead, rather than grabbing whatever was available from day to day.

BUILT FOR A PURPOSE
The mysterious structures at Stonehenge, southern England, *right*, are thought to have been built by our ancestors 4,000 years ago as a form of prehistoric astronomical observatory.

Small hunter-gatherer communities then grew up with women and small children tending to do most of the gathering of foodstuff, while the men and older boys acted as hunters.

But paleoanthropologists think it was not until about 12,000 years ago that humans came to live in more settled communities and began to develop a primitive form of agriculture, growing plants and keeping animals.

FIGURES OF MYSTERY

Experts remain puzzled, however, as to the significance of tiny, carved figurines, known as Venuses, which have been unearthed throughout western Europe and as far east as Siberia. Their exact purpose is unknown, but chances are our ancestors were superstitious and the statuettes were therefore lucky charms, fertility symbols, or representations of a mother goddess, perhaps. Indeed, we know from early graves, where the dead were buried with tools and ornaments, that there was clearly a belief in the afterlife.

Fact file

- It is thought that the first basic use of verbal communication between our ancestors began some two million years ago at the time of *Homo habilis*.

- Flutes made from bone, about 32,000 years old, have been found in France. Music and art distinguish humans from animals and help to keep a social group together.

- Prehistoric families were probably small, rarely exceeding about 10 in total because many children failed to survive infancy due to illness, severe weather conditions, and lack of food.

- Experts believe that the average number of people living in an early pre-agricultural community was probably around thirty.

Challenges

In spite of what microbiologists and paleoanthropologists tell us, can we be sure we humans did indeed evolve from more primitive creatures? Some religious groups still have strong doubts and contest the theory of evolution.

The 19th century saw huge social and scientific changes take place, but there was no greater challenge to traditional beliefs than the theories of English naturalist, Charles Darwin. In his first book, *On the Origin of Species*, published in 1859, he wrote about evolution in relation to the animal kingdom as a whole.

It was his second great work, *The Descent of Man*, however, that was to cause considerable outrage. This time, he had turned his attention to the idea that humans had evolved to their present form rather than having been created as described in the biblical book of *Genesis*. Not unexpectedly, this caused offence among society at large.

According to the *Bible,* God created the world from chaos, completing its form and all life forms, including the first two humans, Adam and Eve, in just six days. Darwin therefore knew his work would be "highly distasteful to many persons," as he put it; but he firmly believed it was his duty to present the theory of evolution for public scrutiny. Even today, creationists (those who believe we were made by God) insist Darwin was wrong and that humans were put on Earth as part of a divine plan.

The descent of man

Charles Darwin, *left*, the 19th century naturalist, presented his theory of evolution in a book with the above title. It was to cause a furor, however, among those who were – and indeed still are – convinced that the biblical version of human history is the correct one.

Indeed, ever since the theory of evolution was first put forward, fundamentalist factions have openly dismissed it as outrageous, casting aside what they claim is Darwin's idea that we have a direct connection with the apes.

However, contrary to what cartoonists and satirists of the late 19th century also took to be the essence of his theory, nowhere in *The Descent of Man* did Darwin actually state that humans are descendants of the apes. Instead, he put forward the notion that humans had been through the same evolutionary processes as other creatures, and that we are only related to apes in that we share a common ancestor.

For many years public concern over Darwin's theory of evolution continued both in England and overseas.

DIVIDED OPINION
As you look at the photograph shown *right*, consider that some believe life on our planet is unique in the universe. Others, meanwhile, whether agreeing with the theory of evolution or not, think there is every likelihood others like us do exist somewhere else in outer space. Only if we exchange signals or actually reach them will we ever know for sure.

In 1925, for instance, the United States became gripped by the trial of a young science teacher from Tennessee, John Thomas Scopes, charged with violating the Butler Act, which forbade schools to teach the subject of evolution.

The trial, which fascinated the whole of North America at the time, centered on whether the biblical story of our creation can be taken literally. Finally, Scopes was fined $100 (a very large sum of money then) for teaching that humans are descended directly from the apes, even though, strictly speaking, Darwin himself had never made that assertion.

Whether you agree with Charles Darwin or prefer to take the creationist view, what paleoanthropologists and microbiologists have found

Fact file

- According to some schools of thought today, belief in a supreme Creator does not automatically negate Darwin's theory of evolution.

- Darwin was not the first person to argue that humans and apes share an ancestor. In 1619, an Italian, Lucilio Vanini, was burned at the stake in France for suggesting this.

- According to the theory of evolution, no plant nor animal (including humans) will remain exactly the same as it is now. But such changes usually occur very slowly, so only many generations ahead will our descendants be able to tell how they have evolved from 21st-century human beings by comparing their DNA with ours, or by studying anatomical photographs.

cannot be ignored. It is a debate that will no doubt continue for many generations to come.

SAVING HUMANITY

Might the days of *Homo sapiens sapiens* – the whole of humankind – be numbered? Or could there be some way we can cooperate to keep our species on an even keel? Recent scientific research, it seems, may have an answer. Perhaps we shall even live forever.

Statistics show that with each passing year, in most developed parts of the world, the average age to which we humans live is increasing. A better diet and superior health care are the principal reasons for this. Yet there are still parts of the globe where epidemics and poor nutrition mean people may not live to celebrate their fortieth birthdays, perhaps even dying at a far younger age.

But there are other problem areas too. Modern warfare, for instance, is a constant threat as many of the world's countries strive to build up nuclear arsenals that could destroy our species entirely.

PERISH THE THOUGHT!
Might an accidental nuclear explosion like the one shown *left*, or atomic warfare, one day exterminate our species?

KILLER DISEASES
In the 17th century a plague spread by rats caused the death of countless people in Europe. Today, too, worldwide, there are equally deadly viruses for which we have yet to find a means of prevention and a cure.

Overpopulation, too, is seen by many as a grave future possibility, bringing with it extreme economic hardship. Experts have even calculated that at the present rate of increase, the number of world citizens could double within two hundred years. Yet at the same time a considerable number of advances are being made, particularly on the health front.

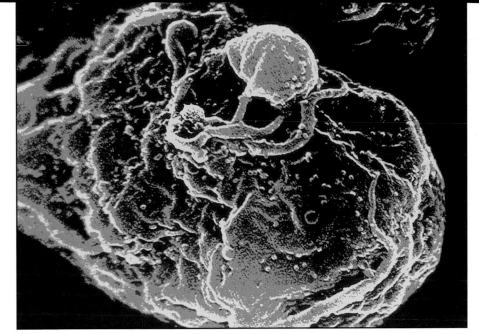

WORLDWIDE EPIDEMIC
One of the most life-threatening diseases of our times is full-blown AIDS, spread by the HIV virus, shown under a microscope *above*.

NEW ORGANS FOR OLD

Back in the 1960s, South African surgeon Dr. Christiaan Barnard made headline news when he became the first person to carry out a heart transplant on a human. Many other surgeons throughout the world have since gone on to perform similar successful operations; but at present, replacement hearts have to come from the victims of accidents who carry cards to indicate they are willing to donate their organs on death. However, will many body parts, including the heart, one day be grown to order?

Provided that such parts can be genetically engineered so that the recipient's body does not reject them, it could possibly become a normal part of medicine to be treated with all sorts of replacement organs.

HERE FOR ETERNITY?

Scientists have even suggested the day may not be so far off when individual human beings can double the normal current lifespan. Perhaps we shall even be able to live forever. Gene therapy, a new form of medical technology, has the potential to cure many diseases, as well as halting the aging process.

But would most people, if offered the chance, opt to extend their lives indefinitely? If they did, surely the world would become even more severely overpopulated?

ENTIRELY ACCEPTABLE?
Not everyone approved when genetic engineers cloned a sheep, seen with her offspring, *left*. Experiments are now even taking place with the cloning of humans.

Fact file

- Through genetic engineering, extending the length of human life to 120 years or more will almost certainly become feasible. Some scientists have even suggested a far longer future life span.

- In 1994 two men were tried for stealing and trying to sell genetic material, which might have been useful in treating damaged human kidneys, from an American laboratory.

- Some people believe that humans may already have been cloned by visitors to this planet from outer space who have performed operations on people and taken some of their tissue and organs.

- A tiny sample of blood or hair might provide enough genetic material to create a clone.

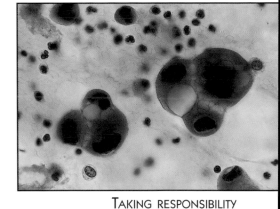

TAKING RESPONSIBILITY
There is no guarantee, but by eating a sensible diet and not smoking, we may overcome the risk of developing cancerous cells, shown *above*.

Recent advances in cloning technology, meanwhile, have left many wondering whether there could be dreadful risks in taking the creation of animal clones one step further and working with humans. Progress often harbors hidden dangers.

43

FUTURE MAN

Assuming that *Homo sapiens sapiens* does manage to survive the scourges of time, will we still look the same after many thousands of generations? The most likely scenario is that we will adapt and evolve according to needs brought about by environmental change.

Let's take a huge leap to the year 500,000 and imagine how, if conditions here on Earth become extreme by then, we may change in appearance and behavior, either naturally or by our own hands.

If global warming continues at a rapid pace, for example, we might start to develop a thick, scaly skin for protection against harmful ultraviolet rays that would seep through huge holes in the ozone layer.

We might also start to grow a sail on our backs, just like those some dinosaurs sported, to aid temperature control. A spiked tail and retractable claws, meanwhile, might provide good built-in defense weapons for use against alien invaders; webbed feet would help to keep us buoyant when swimming; and smaller nostrils and ears might develop flaps as coverings if we ever had to live mostly underwater.

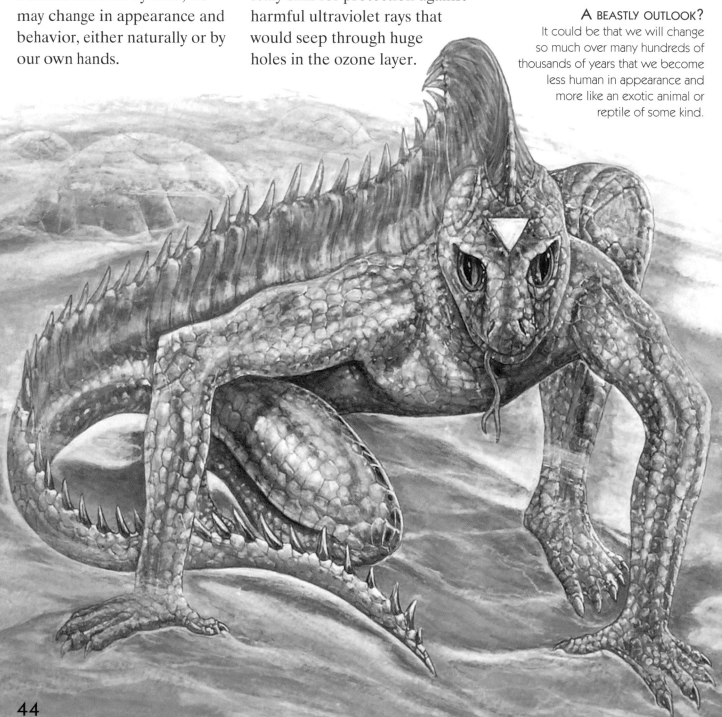

A BEASTLY OUTLOOK?
It could be that we will change so much over many hundreds of thousands of years that we become less human in appearance and more like an exotic animal or reptile of some kind.

It is also perhaps not beyond the bounds of possibility that one day scientists might be able to install computer chips within our brains to help us think at high speed or to enable us to become polyglots (people speaking several tongues), without the need to spend years mastering lots of languages.

We might simply think of a sentence in our native tongue and press a button, so that out would come the words in Russian, Swahili, or whatever language we chose.

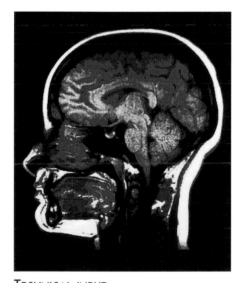

TECHNICAL INPUT
This scan shows the human brain which scientists might one day program with the sum of human knowledge so that study becomes unnecessary.

Our eyes, meanwhile, could perhaps be adapted so that special lenses would help us see when it is pitch dark. We might even be fitted with special motorized wings that would enable us to fly.

MAN OR SUPERMAN?
Over the millennia perhaps we will all develop outstanding levels of intelligence, making us all as brilliant as Albert Einstein, *left*, the greatest scientist who ever lived.

Over tens of thousands of years the dimensions of the hominid skull have increased slowly but surely, to such an extent that we are now set apart from the rest of the animal kingdom mainly because of brain size and intelligence.

With every passing year, what was once merely the stuff of science fiction becomes more of a feasibility. It has been suggested in all seriousness, for example, that it may one day be possible, through insertion of an artificial womb, for men to give birth; or that women could perhaps produce sperm artifically so that men no longer play any part at all in pregnancy. In thousands of years we may even be able to breed babies *outside* the human body. Such possibilities are mind-blowing. Indeed, scientists can only hazard a guess as to what the future will ultimately hold for hominids.

BLAST OFF!
If we succeed in traveling far into outer space, we may have to develop physical features that will suit prevailing conditions outside our solar system.

Fact file

- Even if the present rate of increase slows down, by 2050 the world's population will probably have reached over 11 billion. This may be far too many people for the planet to feed and sustain.

- If, as some scientists have warned, Earth may be destroyed either because the Sun dies or due to asteroid impact, with luck we may be able to escape to another part of the universe. But survival there may require considerable physical adaptation.

- Just as there have been very distinctive hominid species in the past, so in the future we humans may diversify according to local needs. Indeed, there may be many different types of hominids in the distant future.

GLOSSARY

Aborigine
an original inhabitant of Australia

anatomy
study of the structure of the human body

ancestor
a member of your family (or the human species) who lived before you

anthropology
the study of different races of human beings and their behavior

bipedal
walking on two legs

carnivore
a meat-eater

clone
a living creature made from a cell of its parent, to whom it will be genetically identical

concave
curving inward

cranium
part of the skull enclosing the brain

creationist
someone who believes we were created according to biblical tradition

eons
ages

evolution
development through an ancestral line

evolutionist
someone who believes in the theory of evolution

fluoride
a type of mineral

forebear
an ancestor

gait
the way someone walks

gene
a coded message stored in DNA

genetic engineering
the changing of genes artifically

genus
a group of closely related species

herbivore
a plant-eater

insectivore
an insect-eater

microbiologist
someone who studies tiny oganisms

mural
a wall-painting

mutation
a sudden change in a gene

naturalist
an expert in natural history

nomadic
wandering

nucleus
the microscopically small, central part of a body cell

observatory
a place for studying the solar system and distant stars

omnivore
a creature that eats both plants and meat

paleoanthropologist
a scientist who studies the origins of the human species

pigmentation
coloring

plague
a disease

poaching
killing and taking animals illegally

quadrupedal
walking on four limbs

quest
a search

retractable
able to be brought back

skeptic
someone who doubts a theory

A

abominable snowman 9: 34
acid rain 1: 32-33; see also
  pollution
addax 1: 13
adder's tongue 8: 37
Aegyptopithecus 10: 26
Aepyornis 5: 44-45
aetosaurs 2: 11
Afghanistan 4: 29
Africa 3: 21, 41, 45; 4: 8-9. 10-11,
  14, 26, 29; 8: 32; 9: 8-9, 11, 12-
  13, 14-15, 16-17, 18-19, 24, 32-
  33, 39
  northern 1: 12-13, 16, 18, 25,
    27, 28-29, 35, 43; 2: 13, 21, 26-
    27; 6: 14; 10: 10-11, 26-27; see
    also individual countries
  southern 1: 22, 25, 27, 28-29,
    35, 43; 2: 11, 13, 21; 3: 15, 31;
    6: 14, 34-35; 9: 12-13; 10: 10-
    11, 28-29; see also individual
    countries
Aharoni, Prof. I. 1: 40-41
AIDS virus 1: 18-19, 46;
albatross 10: 21
algal blooms 1: 31
Algeria 10: 27
alligators 1: 29; see also Volume 7,
  Reptiles and Amphibians
almas 9: 11
amber 3: 9; 8: 26-27
Ambulocetus 8: 29; 6: 32
America, Central 1, 35; 10: 14-15;
  see also individual countries
  North 1: 7, 9, 12, 15, 16-17, 19,
    22-23, 25, 30, 33, 35, 37, 44-45;
    2: 8, 11, 13, 18, 20-21, 22, 28-
    29, 33, 34, 36, 39; 3: 10-11, 17,
    20, 23, 25, 26-27, 34-35, 40, 42-
    43. 44-45; 4: 15, 21, 22-23; 5:
    14-15, 19, 24-25, 28-29, 36-37,
    38-39, 42-43; 6: 31; 7: 40-41,
    43; 8: 15, 16-17, 23, 24, 30, 32,
    37; 9: 27, 33, 35; 10: 10, 12-13;
    see also Canada
  South 1: 27, 29; 2: 10, 12-13; 3:
    20, 31, 35; 4: 15, 23; 5: 39; 6:
    13, 14-15, 20; 7: 45; 8: 36; 10:
    10, 18-19; see also individual
    countries
ammonites 6: 28-29
amphibians
  see individual species and
  Volume 7, Reptiles and
  Amphibians
Andrews, Prof. M. 4: 35
  R.C. 2: 28; 3: 21, 34-35
Andrewsarchus 8: 29
Andrias scheuchzeri 7: 16-17
Anning, M. 6: 10, 22-23
Antarctic 3: 31; 6: 15; 10: 20-21
Antarctosaurus 10: 21
anteaters, spiny 4: 33
Apatosaurus 10: 15
apes 2: 26-27
Archaeopteryx 3: 8; 5: 8-9; 10: 41
archelons 6: 24-25; 7: 32
archosaurs 7: 15
Arctic 1: 11, 42; 4: 15; 10: 20-21
Ardipithicus ramidus 9: 9
Argentina 3: 20, 35; 5: 10-11; 10:
  19
art, prehistoric 2: 25; 9: 26-27, 39
Arthrolycosa 8: 29
arthropods 6: 24-25; 8: 31
Asia 1: 16, 27, 28, 35; 2: 20, 27,
  29, 39, 42; 4: 20, 26; 9: 8,
  11, 18-19, 20-21, 23; see also
  individual countries
asses 4: 28-29; 10: 33
asteroids 1: 8-9, 32, 37; 8: 8
Atelopus varius 7: 31
Audubon, J. J. 5: 15, 36
auk, great 5: 18-19
aurochs 1: 25; 4: 18-19
Australia 1: 13, 19, 22-23, 28; 2:
  44-45; 3: 13, 15, 24-25, 45; 5:
  34-35; 6: 8-9, 13; 7: 45; 8: 14-
  15, 20, 41; 9: 27, 33, 34; 10: 11,
  22-23
Australopithecus 9: 12-13, 14-15;
  10: 28
Austria 10: 42
aye-aye 1: 42

B

badlands 3: 20-21
Baldwin, D. 3: 42-43
Baluchitherium
  see Indricotherium
bandicoots 4: 42-43
Bangladesh 8: 21
Barapasaurus 10: 30

Darnard, Dr. C. 9: 43
Baryonyx 2: 15; 3: 25; 10: 39
Basilosaurus 6: 32-33
Batrachognathus 7: 12
bats 8: 8; 10: 43
bears 1: 7, 43; 2: 24-25; 3: 15;
  4: 14-15; 10: 20
beavers, giant 4: 44-45; 10: 13
beetles 1: 11, 41; 8: 9, 36-37, 43
Belarus 1: 27
Belgium 6: 16; 9: 22
Bering, V. 5: 40
Bermuda 1: 41
Bigfoot 9: 35
bilbies 4: 43
biostratigraphy 3: 17
birds
  see individual species and
  Volume 5, Extinct Birds
bison 1: 25; 10: 36
Boise, C. 9: 13
Bolivia 2: 15; 10: 19
Bone Wars 3: 26-27
Borneo 1: 27
Bos sauveli 4: 24-25
Brachiosaurus 3: 45; 10: 27
Brazil 1: 25, 39; 7: 44-45; 8: 37;
  10: 17, 19
Brea, La 2: 21
British Isles
  see Great Britian
Brontotherium 2: 38-39
Broom, R. 9: 12-13
Buckland, Revd. W. 9: 25
buckyballs 1: 9
Buffalo Bill 1: 25
Buller, Sir W. 5: 16-17, 23
butterflies 1: 35; 8: 14-15, 20, 33;
  10: 39

C

cactus 8: 19, 22
cahow 1: 41
caiman 7: 44-45
Cambodia 4: 24
camels 1: 12, 39
Canada 1: 25, 27, 33; 2: 17; 5: 3:
  17; 24-25, 45; 4: 15; 6: 13, 30
  31; 9: 35; 10: 12-13; see also
  North America
Canary Islands 8: 18
captive breeding 1: 41; 10: 39
caracara 5: 32-33
caribou 1: 7; 10: 20
Carnotaurus 10: 19
Casteroides 4: 45
cave bears 2: 24-25
  paintings 2: 25; 3: 15; 4: 13;
    9: 26-27, 39
caves 1: 11; 3: 14-15
centipedes 8: 30-31
cephalopods 6: 28
Ceratosaurus 7: 24
CFCs 1: 35, 46
Chad 10: 27
chalicotheres 4: 26-27
Chalicotherium 4: 26-27
chichid 10: 19
Chile 6: 31, 44
chimpanzees 2: 27; 9: 30-31
China 9, 16, 25; 2: 11, 27, 33,
  36, 43; 3: 15, 25, 32, 35, 37, 45;
  4: 15; 8: 15; 9: 11, 20-21, 33;
  10: 34
Chipko Movement 8: 22
chondrichthians 6: 18
chordates 6: 19
cisco 6: 20
clam, giant 8: 40
Clark, General W. 3: 43
Classopolis 8: 17
climate change 1: 34-35, 37; see
  also global warming, Ice Ages
cloning 9: 43; 10: 31
clubmoss 8: 13
coal 3: 9; 8: 8-9, 15
cockroaches 8: 30-31
coelacanth 1: 41; 6: 34-35; 7: 39
Coelophysis 2: 13, 15; 3: 42
Coelosauravus 7: 10
Columbus, C. 6: 38-39
condors 1: 45; 10: 13
conservation 1: 27, 29, 43, 44-45;
  see also individual species,
  national parks
Cook, Capt. J. 1: 20; 5: 17, 31;
  8: 38; 9: 37; 10: 25
Cope, E. D. 3: 26-27
coprolites 2: 15, 33
  see also trace fossils
coral 6: 42-43; 10: 22
  see also Great Barrier Reef, reefs

cormorants 1: 30; 5: 40 41
corncrake 10: 43
Corsica 4: 30-31
Cortés, H. 8: 40
Costa Rica 2: 21; 10: 14-15
cotton mouse 10: 13
Cotylorhyncus 7: 21
cougar 1: 44
cowry, white-toothed 8: 41
crabs 6: 13
crane, Japanese 1: 43
creation theory 9: 40-41
Crick, F. 9: 30
Cro-Magnons 2: 19, 24; 9: 24-25
cross-breeding 1: 39; see also
  hybrids
cryogenics 8: 45
Cryptocleidus 6: 16
Cuba 10: 17
cuckoos 10: 38
Cuvier, G. 2: 36; 4: 27; 7: 16
cycads 8: 17
Czech Republic 6: 13; 10: 43

D

Dactylis 8: 45
damselflies 1: 21
Dart, R. 9: 12-13, 32
Darwin, C. 2: 30, 41; 4: 16-17;
  6: 42; 8: 37; 9: 12, 37, 20-41
Dawson, C. 9: 36-37
Dawson's caribou 1: 25, 28
Dear Boy 9: 13
deer 1: 7; 10: 33, 35
deforestation 1: 7, 26- 27, 34;
  8: 18; 10: 14, 16-17, 18, 31
Deinogalerix 4: 36-37
dendrochronology 3: 29
Denmark 4: 15
desertification 1: 6, 34-35, 45
Desmatosuchus 2: 11
Diadaphorus 2: 31
Dilophosaurus 2: 14-15
Dimetrodon 7: 12-13; 6: 17
Dinictis 2: 20
dinosaurs 1: 6; 2: 10, 12-13,
  14-15, 16-17; 6: 17; 8: 15; see
  also individual species
Diprotodon 2: 44-45; 10: 23
diprotodonts 2: 44-45
disasters, natural
  see drought, earthquakes,
  famine, floods, volcanoes
discoveries, new 1: 38-39
diseases 1: 18-19, 21, 27, 31, 33,
  46; 9: 42-43
DNA 4: 35; 8: 27
dodo 5: 12-13; 8: 8
Dominican Republic 8: 26-27; 10:
  16-17
donkey 1: 39
Dorudon 6: 32; 10: 26
Douglass, E. 3: 11
dragonflies 8: 24-25
Dromiceiomimus 3: 11
drought 1: 6, 10-11, 22
dryopithecines 2: 27
Dsungeripterus 2: 36
ducks 5: 24-25
dugong 6: 37
Dunkleosteus 3: 31; 6: 19, 40
Dusicyon australis 4: 17

E

eagle, bald 1: 45
earthquakes 1: 16-17; 10: 9, 11
earwigs 8: 34-35
Easter Island 8: 8, 38-39
echidna 4: 33
echium 8: 18
Ecuador 1: 45; 8: 19
Edaphosaurus 7: 20
Edmontosaurus 2: 17
eggs 3: 34-35; 7: 9
Egypt 6: 33; 10: 26-27
Elasmosaurus 6: 10-11
elephant birds 4: 11; 5: 44-45
elephants 2: 18, 31, 35
  dwarf 4: 10-11
elk 1: 7; 10: 39
England
  see Great Britain
Eoraptor 3: 20
endangered species 1: 42-43; see
  also individual species
Entelodon 10: 30
equator 10: 29
Equus
  see asses, horses
Eritrea 4: 29
erosion 1: 46; see also
  desertification

Eryops 7: 9
Erythrosuchus 7: 8
Ethiopia 4: 29; 9: 9, 14-15
Eudimorphodon 10: 44
Euparkeria 2: 11
Eurhinosaurus 6: 23
Europe 1: 33; 2: 11, 20, 23, 27; 3:
  30; 6: 8-9, 13, 25, 26; 4: 15, 19,
  20, 23; 8: 19, 24, 26-27; 9: 18,
  27, 39, 42; 10: 10
  central 10: 42-43
  northern 10: 40-41
  southern 10: 44-45
  see also individual countries
Eusthenopteron 6: 19
evolution 1: 46; see also Darwin, C.
extinctions, mass 1: 32, 36-37; 8: 8
  rate of 1: 45; see also individual
  species and Volume 1, Why
  Extinction Occurs

F

Falkland Islands 4: 16-17
Falklands fox
  see foxes
famine 1: 37
Far East 10: 34-35
fashion 1: 28-29
ferns 8: 17; see also plants
fires 1: 22-23; 5: 35
fish 1: 12-13, 30, 33; 6: 18-19,
  20-21, 45; 10: 13, 15, 19, 25
  see also individual species
flickers 5: 29
  see also woodpeckers
floods 1: 34-35, 36-37; 7: 17
foods, genetically modified 8: 21
footprints 3: 12-13; 6: 17
forests 8: 12-13; see also rain
  forests, woodlands
fossil fuel
  see coal, gas, oil
  Grove 8: 12-13
  hunting 3: 20-21, 22-23
  record 3: 30-31
  site, visiting a 3: 10-11
fossils, collecting 3: 18-19, 20-21,
  22-23, 24-25
  dating of 3: 16-17
  formation of 3: 8-9
  index 3: 31
  laboratory work on 3: 38-39
  unearthing 3: 32-33
foxes 4: 16-17; 10: 20
France 2: 18, 25, 27; 3: 15, 34-35;
  9: 22-23, 24, 26-27, 29, 33; 10:
  41, 44-45
frogs 1: 19; 7: 9, 31, 42-43
Fuller, E. 5: 19

G

Gaia 8: 9
Galápagos Islands 7: 33, 44-45
Gambia 6: 31
gas 8: 11
Gasaurus 3: 32-33
gastropods 8: 28-29
gastroliths 2: 16-17; 5: 31
gaur 10: 31
gavial 10: 30
Gavialis ganeticus 7: 15
gecko 7: 37
Gemuendina 6: 18
gentians 1: 10
Genyornis 10: 23
Germany 2: 13, 18, 36; 3: 8, 45; 5:
  8-9; 6: 27; 7: 41; 9: 22-23; 10:
  40-41
gibbons 10: 35
Gibraltar 3, 31
Gila monster 1: 44
ginkgo biloba 8: 16
Giraffatian 7: 15; 10: 27
Gigantopithecus 3: 15
glaciers 1: 11
global warming 1: 34-35; 6: 43; 10:
  20-21
  see also climate change
Glyptodon 2: 40
goats 1: 20; 4: 12-13
Gondwana 8: 15; 10: 8
gorillas 2: 27
Gray's monitor lizard 1: 41
grayling 10: 25
Great Barrier Reef 6: 31, 42
  see also Australia, coral

Great Britain 1: 18-19, 45; 2: 13,
  37; 3: 22-23, 25, 30-31, 33, 36-
  37, 43, 44-45; 6: 10-11, 12-13,
  21; 7: 43; 8: 12-13, 31, 33, 37;
  9: 36, 39; 10: 38-39
Greece 1: 33; 10: 45
greenhouse effect 1: 34
  see also climate change
Grey's wallaby 4: 38-39
grosbeak, Kona 1: 21
ground sloth, giant 3: 13
Guadelupe 5: 29, 32-33, 35; 10,
  14-15

H

habitat destruction 1: 26-27; see
  also deforestation
hadrosaurs 3: 13
Hainosaurus 6: 16
Hallucigenia 8: 29
hamster, golden 1: 40-41
hare-wallabies 4: 43
Hawaii 1: 20-21, 39
heath hens 5: 38-39
hedgehogs 4: 36-37
Herrerasaurus 2: 13
Heyerdahl, T. 8: 39
hibiscus 1: 21
hoatzin 5: 9
hog, pygmy 1: 41
hominids
  see individual species and
  Volume 9, Hominids
Homo diluvii testis 7: 16
  erectus 9: 18-19, 34
  habilis 9: 16-17
  sapiens sapiens 9: 25, 30-31,
    38-39, 42-43, 44-45
Homotherium 2: 21
honeycreepers 1: 21; 5: 42-43;
  8: 8
honeyeaters 1: 21
Horner, J. 3: 34
horses 1:15; 2: 43; 3: 40-41;
  4: 20-21, 29; 9: 29
horsetails 8: 14-15
huia 10: 25
humans, survival of 1: 44-45
  see also Homo sapiens sapiens
Hungary 10: 43
hunting 1: 24-25, 42-43, 45;
  9: 28-29; 10: 21, 27, 35
  see also individual species
hutias 10: 16
Huxley, T.H. 3: 43
hybrids 8: 20-21
Hydrodamalis gigas 6: 37
Hylonomus 7: 36
Hyperodapedon 7: 39
Hyracotherium 4: 21

I

ibex 10: 45
ibis, flightless 1: 21
Icarosaurus 7: 10
Ice Ages 1: 10-11; 2: 19, 21, 22-
  23, 24; 8: 16
ichthyosaurs 3: 22; 6: 22-23
Ichthyostega 7: 8-9
iguana 1: 22, 44-45
Iguanodon 3: 36-37, 43
inbreeding 1: 44
India 1: 18, 41, 42; 2: 11, 23, 27;
  3: 31, 35; 5: 24-25, 39; 7: 44; 8:
  22; 10: 30-31
Indonesia 1, 27; 9: 18, 20
Indricotherium 2: 42
insects 1: 45; see also individual
  species and Volume 8,
  Invertebrates and Plants
invertebrates
  see Volume 8, Invertebrates
  and Plants
Iran 4: 29; 10: 32-33
Iraq 3: 15; 4: 28; 10: 32-33
Ireland, Northern
  see Great Britain
Israel 1: 9; 5: 25; 6: 10, 30; 7: 42-
  43; 9: 23; 10: 32-33
  see also Middle East
Italy 3: 28; 9: 23; 10: 44`

J

Janensch, Dr. W. 3: 45
Japan 1: 9; 4: 23; 10: 34-35
Japanese crane 1: 43

Java 9: 18, 20
Man 9: 20-21
Jefferson, T. 3: 43
Johanson, D. 9: 14-15
Jordan 10: 32-33
ungle
see deforestation, rain forests

K
Kamptobaatar 2: 32
Kenya 9: 16-17, 18-19; 10: 28
Kew Gardens 8: 44-45
keystone species 1: 37, 45
kiwis 10: 24
Komodo dragon 7: 23, 36
Korea 5: 25; *see also* Far East
kouprey 4: 24-25
Kronosaurus 6: 8-9
Kuehnosaurus 7: 10
Kumar, Prof. A. 9: 14-15

L
aboratory work 3: 38-39
abyrinthodont 10: 23
adybugs 8: 42
agomorph 4: 30
Lagorchestes 4: 39
Lagosuchus 2: 10
Lakes, A. 3: 27
angurs 10: 35
Latimer, M. Courtenay- 6: 34-35
Laurasia 10: 8
Leakey family. 9: 9, 13, 16-17
Leguat, F. 5: 26-27
eopards 1: 29; 8: 37
Lepidodendron 8: 13
ligron 1: 39
Linnaeus, C. 1: 39; 8: 36
ions 2: 44-45; 4: 39; 10: 45
itopterns 2: 30-31
iving fossils 7: 38-39; *see also* coelacanth
izards 7: 9, 10-11, 36-37
Longisquama 7: 10
orises 10: 35
Lucy 9: 14-15
ynx, Spanish 1: 26

M
macaques 10: 35
Machairodus 2: 21
Macrauchenia 2: 30-31
Macrotherium 4: 27
Madagascar 1: 22, 26, 42; 3: 33; 5: 44-45; 7: 43, 44; 8: 37; 10: 28-29
Maiasaura 3: 34
maidenhead trees 8: 16
Majorca 4: 12-13
Makela, B. 3: 34; *see also* Spain
Malaysia 1: 27
mammals
see individual creatures and Volume 4, *Extinct Mammals*
Mamenchisaurus 7: 28
mammoths 1: 10; 2: 18-19, 22; 3: 9, 33; 10: 39
mamo 5: 42-43
man-beasts 9: 34-35
manatees 1: 19, 43; 6: 36
mandrills 1: 24
mangroves 8: 18
Mantell family. 3: 43
Marsh, O.C. 3: 26-27, 37, 42; 6: 11
marsupials 2: 32-33, 44-45; *see also* individual creatures
Massospondylus 10: 29
Mauritius 5: 12-13; 8: 8-9; 10: 29
medicines 1: 44-45; 7: 27
Medullosa 8: 15
Megalania 7: 36-37
Megalosaurus 3: 36
megamouth 1: 39
Meganeura 8: 24
Megantereon 2: 21
Megatherium 2: 35
Megazostrodon 10: 28
Meiolania 7: 32
Melanosaurus 2: 13
mermaids 9: 35
Merychippus 4: 21
Mesohippus 3: 40-41; 4: 21; 10: 13
mesonychids 2: 28-29
Mesonyx 2: 28; 10: 12
Mesosaurus 6: 14-15
Metamynodon 2: 43
Metasequoia 8: 15
Mexico 1: 44; 4: 14-15; 8: 19, 41; 10: 14; *see also* America, Central
Microgoura meeki 5: 21
Middle East 4: 28; 9: 24-25; 10: 32-33; *see also* individual countries
Millennium Seed Bank 8: 44-45
millipedes 8: 31
mink, sea 10: 13
missing link 9: 10-11, 31, 36-37
mistakes, famous 3: 36-37
Mixosaurus 6: 23
moas 1: 21; 5: 30-31; 10: 23, 24
Mongolia 2: 15, 28-29, 32, 43; 3: 21, 34-35, 45; 4: 21, 29
monsoons 1: 13
monkeys 1: 41; 10: 14, 26-27, 35; *see also* chimpanzees, mandrills, orangutans
monotremes 4: 33
Moravamlacris 8: 31
Moropus 4: 27
morphology 3: 28-29
mosasaurs 6: 16
moths 8: 37
multituberculates 2: 32-33
mummification 3: 9
Muraeonosaurus 6: 11; 7: 29
muskrat, West Indian 1: 7, 14
Mussaurus 2: 12-13; 3: 25
mutations 1: 27, 46
Muttaburrasaurus 3: 24; 10: 23
myxomotosis 1: 18

N
naming species 1: 39
national parks 1: 7, 45; 10: 12-13, 41
Native American Indians 1: 25
Neanderthals 2: 19, 24-25; 3: 15, 30; 9: 22-23, 24-25, 35; 10: 33
nene 1: 21
Neoglyphes inopinata 1: 41; 8: 41
Neopilina galatheae 8: 40
new species 1: 38-39
see also discoveries, new
New Zealand 3: 43; 5: 16-17, 22-23, 25, 30-31, 39; 6: 16; 8: 37; 10: 11, 34-35
Newfoundland 4: 22
Niger 3: 21, 41
Nilssonia 8: 16
Niño, El 1: 35
Norway 4: 15
Nothomymecia macrops 8: 39
Nothosaurus 6: 16
nuclear testing 1: 39

O
ocelot 10: 13
Ogopogo 6: 30
oil 1: 27, 30-31; 8: 6, 38
okapi 1: 32-33
onager, Syrian 4: 28-29
orangutans 2: 27
orchids 8: 8, 19, 21, 37; 10: 39
Ornicthocheirus 10: 39
Ornithodesmus 2: 37
Ornithomimus 2: 17
oryx, Arabian 1: 25, 43; 10: 33
osteichthians 6: 18
ostracoderms 6: 18
Oviraptor 2: 15; 3: 35
Owen, R. 2: 12, 41; 3: 36-37, 43; 5: 30
owls 1: 21; 5: 22-23
ozone 1: 35, 46; 10: 21

P
Pakicetus 6: 32-33
Pakistan 2: 43; 6: 32-33
Palacophonus 8: 30
Palaeocastor 4: 44-45
Palaeoloxodon 3: 44
paleobotany 3: 28-29
see also Volume 8, Invertebrates and Plants
paleogeography 10: 8-9
paleoichnology 3: 12-13
paleontologists, work of
see fossils
Palestine 4: 28; 7: 42-43
see also Middle East
Palorchestes 2: 44; 10: 23
palynology 3: 28
Panama 1: 19;
pandas 1: 25; 10: 35
Pangaea 2: 13; 10: 8
Panthera leo leo 4: 40-41
Papua New Guinea 5: 20-21; 7: 45; 8: 32
parakeet, Carolina 5: 36-37
Parasaurolophus 7: 24
parasuchia 2: 11
pareiasaurs 7: 18-19
Paraiasaurus 7: 18-19
Parosuchus 7: 15
Pau-brasil 8: 19
Peking Man 9: 20-21
pelicans 1: 31
Peloneustes 6: 8
pelycosaurs 2: 9; 7: 20-21
permafrost 1: 11, 46; 2: 18-19; 3: 9; *see also* Ice Ages
perissodactyl 2: 37, 43
Peteinosaurus 7: 12
petrification 3: 9
Philippines 1: 15, 41; 8: 18, 41
Phobosuchus 6: 17
Phororhacos 5: 10-11
phosphates 1: 31
phyloplankton 8: 11
Phylotillon 4: 27
pigeons 5: 14-15, 20-21
pigs 1: 20; *see also* hog
pika 4: 30-31
Piltdown hoax 3: 3; 9: 36-37
Pithecanthropus 9: 20
piopio 5: 16-17
Placochelys 6: 26
placoderms 6: 19, 31
placodonts 6: 26-27
plant life 1: 15, 45; 2: 17, 33; 10: 18, 42; *see also* individual plants, trees, and Volume 8, *Invertebrates and Plants*
Plastosaurus 6: 9
plate tectonics 1: 16, 46; 10: 9
plateosaurids 10: 41
Plateosaurus 2: 13
Ples, Mrs. 9: 12
plesiosaurs 3: 27; 6: 8, 10-11, 31; 7: 28-29; 10: 34
Pleuracanthus 6: 41
Pliohippus 4: 21
pliosaurs 6: 8-9
Plot, Prof. R. 3: 36-37
poaching 1: 29, 42-43; 10: 43; *see also* hunting
Podopteryx 7: 10
poikilothermic 7: 25
poisoning 1: 7, 45
Polacanthus 3: 25
Poland 2: 22; 4: 18
polar regions 10: 20-21; *see also* Antarctic, Arctic
pollen 1: 11; 3: 28-29
pollution 1: 30-31, 32-33, 35; 6: 20-21, 43, 44; 10: 40, 43; *see also* acid rain; waters, polluted
Polo, M. 4: 11; 5: 44
Polyborus lutosus 5: 32-33
ponderosa pine 1: 22
population, world 1: 37; 9: 42, 35; 10: 31
Portugal 10: 44
Potamotherium 10: 45
potoroos 1: 22
prairie chicken 5: 39; 10: 13
Preodactylus 7: 12
Procompsognathus 2: 13
Proconsul 2: 26; 3: 41; 9: 11
Procoptodon 2: 44-45
Project Hercules 8: 35
Prolagus 4: 31
prosauropods 2: 12-13
Protoceratops 2: 15; 3: 21, 34
protodinosaur 2: 10
protosuchia 2: 11; 7: 8
Protosuchus 7: 8
Przewalski's horse 4: 21
Psaronius 8: 15
pseudosuchia 2: 11
Psittacosaurus 2: 17
Pterodactylus 2: 36
Pterodaustro 7: 13
pterosaurs 1: 37; 7: 12-13; 10: 44
Ptylodus 2: 33
puffins 1: 31

Q
quagga 4: 8-9
quail 10: 25, 31
quelili 10: 15
Quetzalcoatlus 2: 36-37; 7: 12

R
rabbits 1: 18; 10: 14
radioactivity 1: 27
radioisotope dating 3: 17
rafflesia 8: 9
rain forests 1: 24, 33, 35; 8: 9; 10: 15, 18-19; *see also* deforestation, forests
rainfall
see drought, floods, monsoons
Ramapithecus 9: 10-11, 32
rat-rabbit 4: 30-31
reconstructions 3: 40-41
Red List 1: 43
tides 1: 31
rediscoveries 1: 40-41; 8: 38-39, 40-41
reefs 6: 42-43
reptiles
see individual species and Volume 7, *Reptiles and Amphibians*
resin 3: 9
Réunion 5: 12-13, 26-27
rhinos 1: 15, 43; 2: 22-23, 38-39, 43; 3: 32; 10: 41
rhynchosaurs 7: 38-39
rice 8: 21
rimis 9: 35
roc 4: 11
rodents 2: 32
Rodrigues 5: 12-13
Romania 3: 35; 10: 43
Rothschild, Baron L. W. 3: 18; 5: 21, 23, 42-43
Russia 1: 45; 4: 29; 10: 36-37
Rwanda 2: 27

S
saber-tooths 2: 20-21
salamanders 7: 9, 16-17
Saltasaurus 3: 35
Saltopus 2: 13
Sarchosuchus imperator 7: 14-15
Sardinia 4: 30-31
sasquatch 9: 35
sauropods 2: 12, 16-17; 6: 17; 7: 28-29
Scheuchzer, J. J. 7: 16
Scopes, J. T. 9: 41
scorpions 6: 31; 8: 30-31
Scotland
see Great Britain
sculpin 1: 12-13
Scutosaurus 7: 19
sea cows 6: 36-37
daisies 8: 37
levels 1: 34-35
minks 10: 13
monsters 6: 31
otters 1: 45
urchins 1: 45
seals 1: 29; 6: 38-39, 44; 10: 17, 42
seed bank 8: 44-45
Sereno, Prof. P. 3: 21
Seymouria 7: 40-41
sharks 1: 37; 6: 40-41
Sheba, Queen of 1: 12
Shonisaurus 6: 22
Siberia 1: 9; 2: 18-19, 23; 4: 15; 6: 31; 9: 39
Sicily 1: 15; 4: 10-11
Sierra Leone 10: 27
silification 3: 9
Sinanthropus pekinensis 9: 21
Sivapithecus 2: 27; 9: 11
skinks 1: 13; 7: 37
sloths, ground 2: 34-35; 10: 17
Slovakia 10: 43
Slovenia 10: 43
Smilodon 2: 21; *see also* saber-tooths
Smith, Prof. J. L. B. 6: 34
W. W. 5: 22-23
snails 8: 28
snakes 7: 9, 26-27, 44-45; 10: 13, 37
solar power 1: 35
solenodons 10: 17
solitary 5: 26-27
Solomon Islands 5: 20-21
King 1: 12
Sophora toromiro 8: 39
Spain 3: 13; 9: 27, 29; 10: 44-45
speciation, geographical 8: 21
species, new 1: 28-29; *see also* hybrids, redisocoveries
speech 9: 19, 39
spiders 8: 28-29
Spinosaurus 2: 9; 7: 24
squirrels 2: 32; 10: 39
Sri Lanka 10: 31
starling, mysterious 10: 25
Staurikosaurus 2: 12
Stegosaurus 2: 17; 10: 12
Steller, G. 5: 41; 6: 36
Steller's sea cow 6: 36-37
stilt, Hawaiian 1: 21
sturgeon 10: 13
Sudan 10: 27
Sumatra 1: 25; 2: 23
Sweden 1: 27; 10: 27
Switzerland 9: 29; 10: 41
Syria 1: 40; 4: 28-29; 10: 32-33

T
Taeniolabis 2: 33
tamarin, black-faced lion 10: 18
Tanistropheus 6: 17; 7: 28-29
Tanzania 1:18, 27; 9: 9, 14-15
taphonomy 3: 17
tapirs 2: 43
tarpans 4: 21
Tasmania 10: 22-23
Tasmanian tiger 4: 34; 10: 22
Taung baby 9: 12-13
taxonomy 8: 37
Temnodontosaurus 6: 17
Temnospondyls 7: 43
temperature 7: 24-25
Terrestrisuchus 7: 15
thecodonts 2: 10-11
theropods 2: 15
thylacine 4: 34-35; 10: 22
Thylacoleo 2: 44-45
Thylacosmilus 10: 19
Tibet 1: 39; 9: 35
tigers 1: 18, 42, 45; 10: 31, 34, 36; *see also* Tasmanian tiger
Titan longhorn beetle 1: 41
titanosaur 3: 33
Titanus giganteus 8: 46-47
toads 7: 9, 30-31
tools 9: 16-17, 19, 32-33
tortoises 7: 32-33, 34-35, 44-45
trace fossils 2: 16; *see also* coprolites, footprints, tracks
tracks, fossilized 2: 15; 3: 12-13
trade, illegal 7: 34-35; 10: 17
trees 1: 33; 3: 9, 28-29; 8: 8-9, 10-11, 12-13, 14-15, 16-17, 22-23, 26-27, 38-39; *see also* deforestation, forests, plants, rain forests
trematodes 7: 43
Triadobatrachus 7: 43
Triassochelys 6: 25
Trichoplax 8: 41
trilobites 6: 12-13
Tsintaosaurus 3: 37
tuatara 7: 38-39
Tunisia 10: 27
Turkey 1: 45; 6: 30; 10: 45
turtles 6: 35; 7: 32-33, 34-35, 44-45; 10: 45
Tyrannosaurus rex 3: 41

U
Uganda 1: 45; 2: 27
Ukraine 2: 22; 10: 36-37
United Kingdom
see Great Britain
United States
see America, North
uranium 3: 17
Ursus maritimus 4: 15
Uruguay 3: 35

V
Varanasaurus 7: 21
Varanus 7: 23, 36
Velociraptor 10: 37
vents 6: 45
Venuses 9: 39
Vietnam 9: 11, 35; 10: 35
volcanic activity 1: 14-15; 5: 31; 10: 11
vulture, painted 10: 12

W
Wales
see Great Britain
wallabies 4: 38-39
Watson, J. 9: 30
war 10: 33
see also individual countries
weasel 5: 23
Wegener, A. 10: 9
West Indies 1:14, 25, 28; 6: 38-39; 8: 19; 10: 16-17; *see also* individual islands
Western Ghats 10: 20
whales 6: 32-33, 45; 10: 21
whekau 5: 22-23
Wilson, A. 5: 28-29
wisent 10: 37
wolves 4: 22-23; 10: 13, 34, 37
woodlands 10: 38
woodpeckers 5: 28-29; 10: 14
worms 8: 29; 10: 29
wren 10: 25

X
Xphactinus 6: 20

Y
yeti 9: 11, 34-35
Yugoslavia 10: 42-43

Z
Zaglossus 4: 32-33
Zaire 2: 27
zebra 1: 39; 4: 8-9
Zygomaturus 10: 23